**LIBRARY OF CONGRESS
CATALOGING-IN-PUBLICATION DATA**

Beginning your journey: a guide for new professionals in student affairs /
Marilyn J. Amey and Lori M. Reesor, editors.

    p. cm

    Includes bibliographical references

    ISBN 0-931654-30-0

    1. Student affairs services—United States—Handbooks, manuals, etc.
2. Counseling in higher education—Vocational guidance—United States.
3. Student counselors—Training of—United States. I. Amey, Marilyn J. II. Reesor,
Lori M. III. National Association of Student Personnel Administrators (U.S.)
LB2342.9.B45 1998
378.1'94047—dc21   98-37300
                                                CIP

Beginning Your Journey

A GUIDE FOR NEW PROFESSIONALS IN STUDENT AFFAIRS

EXPANDED AND REVISED

MARILYN J. AMEY AND LORI M. REESOR, EDITORS

Other NASPA Monograph Titles

To purchase NASPA publications, call 301-638-1749 or 301-638-1767, or send a fax to 301-843-0159.

Table of Contents

Introduction

" New professionals are the future of our profession." This is a common phrase heard when a seasoned staff member addresses a group of newcomers. Our graduate degree programs concentrate on providing students with the theoretical and practical experiences to help them succeed in the student affairs profession. As we know, however, these graduate programs are diverse in their teachings and emphases. It is crucial that NASPA be an active voice in the development of new professionals, and this monograph is one way of demonstrating that commitment.

The purpose of this monograph is to ease the transition from graduate student to full-time professional and to increase the retention of new professionals in the field. While it is not intended as an administrative cookbook, we examine key issues facing new professionals and ways of thinking about the challenges and opportunities that are embedded in careers in student affairs. Issues facing those entering the profession have a certain degree of comparability, whether one assumes a first professional position or moves into student affairs from another field, and whether one is employed at a community college or in a research university. Understanding organizational culture and its impact on work, thinking through career configurations, reflecting on the aspects of collegiate life that affect the way work unfolds, exploring the values and belief systems of the field are all issues that confront new and newer professionals. At the same time, for those more experienced professionals moving into the student affairs arena for the first time, past employment knowledge and expectations impact perspectives and create a different set of needs and concerns. Given the space limitations of the monograph, we assume a primary readership of entering professionals and seek to capture experiences that entering professionals and those new to the field have in common. To this end, the term "new professional" is used throughout the text. We also assume that supervisors, graduate preparation faculty, and other supporters of new professionals constitute a secondary readership for the monograph, and that they will find utility in a discussion of current pressing issues as seen by new professionals. Finally, while we acknowledge new professionals' work in community colleges, most of our writing is geared toward new professionals in four-year institutions.

In determining those issues most relevant for inclusion in this monograph, it is important for us to begin with a brief contextual discussion of the arena in which student affairs work takes place in the 21st Century. We work and will work in organizations that are both political and multicultural. If new professionals are unaware of the nature of colleges and universities or do not understand the competing priorities that cause institutional members to negotiate for

Understanding organizational culture and its impact on work, thinking through career configurations... and exploring the values and belief systems of the field are all issues that confront new and newer professionals.

resources, they are often adversely affected by organizational politics. In addition to its inherent political culture, many authors chastise the overall higher education system for not achieving a truly multicultural orientation. These same authors simultaneously argue that the future of colleges and universities rests within a multicultural environment (Brazzell, 1996; El-Khawas, 1996; Hurtado, Milem, Clayton-Pedersen, & Allen, 1998; Rhoads & Valadez, 1996; Stage & Manning, 1992). To this end, they call for changes in institutional climate and culture to accommodate an increasingly diverse student population; for increasing the culturally diverse make-up of faculty and staff; for changing institutional directives, statutes, and policies to reflect the realities of a changing clientele; for increased technological expertise and instruction that will accommodate a wider range of learning styles; and for leadership that can guide the academy into a multicultural environment for the 21st Century. We also recognize the extent to which postsecondary institutions are struggling to redefine themselves in the midst of a technological revolution that is changing every aspect of academe: what it means to be an educator, to be a learner, to provide services for students, and even to be a college campus. Although we cannot foresee all the ways in which increased use of technology will transform the practice of student affairs, it is clear that, around the central issues discussed in this monograph, things are changing! New professionals enter student affairs within this press of politics, fundamental philosophic changes, seemingly unlimited innovation, and boundary redefinition, and we write this monograph with these environmental constructs in mind.

We believe, also, in the value of hearing from new professionals themselves. Therefore, personal vignettes and the "talk" of new professionals are woven throughout the monograph to give voice to their concerns, strategies, and beliefs. Sometimes, these voices are those of individual professionals included to illustrate a specific point; other times, the voices are representative amalgams of viewpoints expressed by many. Pseudonyms are used in all cases to protect confidentiality.

Barbara Snyder and Lori McDonald begin the monograph by reflecting on the issues raised in it from the dual perspectives of a new professional and a senior student affairs administrator. In dialogic fashion, Snyder and McDonald add their voices to those of others in the volume who speak directly to challenges facing new professionals and provide support and guidance. Marilyn Amey uses a conceptual model of organizational culture to discuss organizational and political realities confronting new professionals. David Guthrie and Thomas McWhertor consider the implicit values that give form and nuance to administrative practice. They discern these values from four contexts (personal, institutional, professional, and legal) and describe the resulting arena in which one's ethic is framed. Randi Schneider examines the complexities of supervision and the role of the supervisor. Using organizational and leadership theories as guideposts, Schneider analyzes ways in which this relationship is exhibited and provides insights to deal with potential, and often inevitable, dissonance.

Camille Consolvo and Michael Dannells help us think through the issues of collaboration between student affairs professionals and faculty. They highlight challenges and provide useful strategies for cultivating relationships that support seamless student learning. Lori Reesor takes the lead in describing various approaches to professional involvement and networking, inter- and intra-institutionally. She describes avenues for participation and raises awareness of issues associated with cross-gender and cross-cultural support systems. Douglas Toma and Kelly Grady tackle what remains a key component of successful careers in student affairs work—finding life balance. New professionals have much to consider in striking a healthy equilibrium as they strive to excel in aspects of their personal and professional lives. Toma and Grady offer insights and frameworks for thinking through these key decisions and choices. Florence Hamrick and Brian Hemphill take professional development and career planning in a different direction as they explore career paths and advancement opportunities. Hamrick and Hemphill discuss various scenarios, including the role of doctoral study, and present ways of envisioning one's future in the profession.

Finally, Shannon Ellis brings together the reflections of leaders in the profession. We want to honor the words of new professionals themselves throughout the monograph. In the same spirit, we find great value and wisdom in listening to the voices of those leaders who have come before, who helped to shape the profession as we know it today, and whose commitment to student affairs remains as deep and unwavering as when they too were new professionals.

In closing, we are reminded of the advice of one of the leaders in student affairs. Although she wrote them more than a decade ago, Barr's (1989) words of guidance remain stalwart for enjoying work and being an effective student affairs administrator even today, and they serve as a foundation for our monograph: "Enjoy the students"; "Become involved in the institution"; "Maintain perspective"; and "Take time to smell the roses" (p. 525-526).

Note: The contributing authors of this monograph want to express appreciation to the many new professionals across the country who added their stories to our text. Their willingness to share experiences and insights made this a rich experience for us all. Special editorial thanks are extended to W. Judd Hark and Linda Driscoll of Michigan State University, who worked tirelessly with the final editing.

REFERENCES

Barr, M. J. (1993). Becoming successful student affairs administrators. In M. J. Barr & Associates (Eds.), *The handbook of student affairs administration* (pp. 522-529). San Francisco: Jossey-Bass.

Brazzell, J. C. (1996). Diversification of postsecondary institutions. In S. R. Komives, D. B. Woodard, Jr., & Associates (Eds.), *Student services: A handbook for the profession* (3rd ed., pp. 43-63). San Francisco: Jossey-Bass.

El-Khawas, E. (1996). Student diversity on today's campuses. In S. R. Komives, D. B. Woodard, Jr., & Associates (Eds.), *Student services: A handbook for the profession* (3rd ed., pp. 64-80). San Francisco: Jossey-Bass.

Hurtado, S., Milem, J.F., Clayton-Pedersen, A.R., & Allen, W.R. (1998). Enhancing campus climates for racial/ethnic diversity: Educational policy and practice. *Review of Higher Education* 21(3): 279-302.

Rhoads, R. A. & Valadez, J. R. (1996). *Democracy, multiculturalism and the community college: A critical perspective.* New York: Garland Publishing Co.

Stage, F. K. & Manning, K. (1992). *Enhancing the multicultural campus environment: A cultural brokering approach* (New Directions for Student Services No. 60). San Francisco: Jossey-Bass.

CHAPTER 1

Voices of Experience

BARBARA SNYDER AND LORI MCDONALD

Any new professional faces challenges in his or her new role, regardless of the discipline or the particular organization. People drawn to the student affairs profession, whatever their background or experience, are no exception. The support and guidance of experienced professionals is critical to the success of these transitions. Understanding perspectives on educational background, identity, professional development, balance, and the needs of new professionals can assist with the success of individuals in the profession. These transitional issues are addressed by Barbara Snyder, Vice President for Student Affairs at the University of Utah, and Lori McDonald, Assistant Dean of Students and Greek Coordinator at the University of Utah.

This has probably been my biggest challenge as a new professional— figuring out what my job really is and doing it well.

EDUCATIONAL BACKGROUND

Many new professionals come from established graduate preparation programs that emphasize a combination of theory and practice. Often, they are thrust into work situations where their colleagues have not had similar educational experiences and the new professional's effort to utilize this knowledge base is challenged or discounted. Lori McDonald says:

I was so eager to start working that I moved the day after my graduation and took the proverbial "plunge" into the challenges of a full time job. One of the first things I realized was that I was the only staff member with my background of education. I had arrived in a department that employed individuals both with and without master's degrees and not everyone was regularly using student development terminology. I knew that there were a variety of higher education programs out there, but I had not realized that I might be the only one with that exposure to the profession in my first department. This revelation brought me both a sense of surprise and of pride. Likewise, it became a source of both strength and challenge.

New professionals, no matter what their background and education are, need help from student affairs leaders to make sense of their new surroundings, campus culture, professional expectations, and their specific responsibilities.

Many of my colleagues had been in the department for over a decade and had seen it through numerous evolutions and innovations. Others were new to student affairs like me but brought a variety of skill sets from other career paths. We learned to listen to each other and respect the ideas of the team rather than assuming that one person had all of the answers. I had to quickly learn a new software program for managing student records, along with one for managing office operations. I had to learn the policies of the department, along with those of the university as they pertained to my job, my students, and the day-to-day tasks that we all completed. There was a lot to learn before I could imagine how to apply my knowledge of theory to the specific practice of my job.

Barbara Snyder says:

New professionals come to student affairs from all varieties of backgrounds. Some are steeped in traditional graduate preparation programs, but many come from academic disciplines that are peripheral to the core of our activities, but beneficial nonetheless. Department managers will seek to maximize experiences and build working teams drawing from the strengths that individuals bring to tasks and programs. New professionals will achieve the greatest success by taking time and care to learn from their colleagues and to use their own skills to complement, rather than compete, with others. They should pay particular attention to the background and educational experiences of others with whom they work and celebrate those who can help them approach problems or issues in innovative and creative ways. Senior student affairs administrators will appreciate and enhance the experience of those who work collaboratively with others. Effective student affairs programs are those that meld the institutional identity of more seasoned professionals with the enthusiasm and new ideas of new professionals.

IDENTITY

New professionals struggle to find their niche in a working environment, asking themselves "What am I good at? What are my strengths and weaknesses? What do I like and/or dislike about my work?" There is also a struggle to determine where they want to go and how to get there. The supervisor's responsibility is to help new professionals understand the culture of their new communities and focus on the profession, as well as to provide support. Snyder comments:

Most individuals who have achieved a senior role in student affairs can well appreciate the struggle of new professionals to find their professional "home." It is our role to create and maintain the culture of the student affairs organization and to help new colleagues determine where they best fit in it. New professionals will benefit, first and foremost, by completing the job they were hired to do, while looking for additional opportunities to expand their experience and competence. It is rare but appreciated when efforts are made to see the big picture of what the division is working towards, rather than only focusing on one's own area. Since all of what we do in student affairs should connect to student learning, trying to find great separation rather than connecting with other departments and units is counterproductive. Let your supervisor know when you are especially enjoying a particular assignment or when you are especially challenged by a new task so that he or she can provide the support and assistance you need. I always appreciate it when young staff want to know about my career path in the hopes that it will help them find direction. Like almost everyone in student affairs, there is no clear way to the top and all of us can benefit from the wisdom and mistakes of others.

McDonald adds:

Student affairs is not a field that can accurately be described with simplicity. It can be as complicated and diverse as the students with whom we work. New professionals need help in understanding the rich culture of our new community, both on the campus level and at that of the profession at large. What I realized after time and changing positions was that there are parts of every job that I do not necessarily like and that it is impossible to know what the job really is, no matter how much preparation is done for the interview. This has probably been my biggest challenge as a new professional—figuring out what my job really is and how to do it well. Not all supervisors have the time or the willingness to assist a new professional with this challenge. What we need is the encouragement to ask, "What is my job?" and the support to try different roles and tasks to see what it is that we really like to do. This is the only way that we will truly know what we want to continue doing and in what direction to take our careers forward in the profession.

PROFESSIONAL DEVELOPMENT

New professionals must find a way to make a personal commitment to development. Often this means identifying appropriate (and affordable) professional opportunities, looking for creative funding sources, submitting program or research proposals for acceptance at state, regional, or national conferences, etc. Senior administrators who believe in professional development must be supportive of new professionals while balancing the needs of other staff along with other fiscal priorities, especially in times of budget constraints. McDonald recalls:

Professional development was a "buzz word" that I heard early in my graduate program. I quickly joined professional associations and looked for opportunities to make presentations, build relationships with people already in the field, and keep informed about new developments in practice.

When I started my first job, I was faced with fitting a commitment to professional development into a very narrow budget and an extremely hectic schedule of student appointments, planning meetings, and paperwork. What helped me immensely was a director who suggested presenting at a regional conference since travel costs were lower and the meeting was shorter than the national event. Even more beneficial has been a vice president who brought the development opportunities to me on my own campus. Hearing leaders in the profession speak during presentations for the entire division has been inspiring, informative, and extremely accessible.

I have also learned that professional development is not just associations and people outside of my university. There are numerous opportunities for building my skills and developing partnerships within my own campus community. Committee work at all levels of the organization can be an excellent way to capitalize on these opportunities. When my supervisors have the confidence in me to represent the department on various projects, it not only builds my confidence; it contributes to my development as a team member and a professional.

Says Snyder:

It's no secret that we didn't enter the student affairs profession to become wealthy, at least in a financial sense. With typical low starting salaries and colleges and universities increasingly facing budget constraints, it is not easy for new professionals to find the resources they need to support their own professional development. I worked for over 11 years in the field before I received enough professional development money to cover the cost of attending even a regional conference. But those who will advance the most quickly and have the most rewarding careers are those who stay abreast of issues, programs, people, and events on the local, regional, and national scene. With so many on-line services and information sources available today, and so many associations providing e-learning opportunities, it is critical for new professionals to invest time and energy into ongoing professional education. I advise new staff to become involved in associations connected to their own work area, as well as one of the associations leading the student affairs field. Volunteering and sharing your expertise can lead to making professional contacts, which will help you in all of your career endeavors. Ask your supervisor or other colleagues about opportunities for professional development on your own campus and beyond. And, yes, you will likely need to plan your finances to cover some level of your involvement, at least initially. It will be well worth the investment during your career.

MAKING CONNECTIONS AND FINDING BALANCE

New professionals must develop a persona separate from their undergraduate or graduate student role. They are often building a new life in a new place while starting a new job; undoubtedly this becomes overwhelming. Knowing when to take time for themselves, trying to connect across the department, program, campus, and community, and establishing healthy behaviors all create tremendous burdens.

Snyder comments:

One of the greatest challenges for new professionals is finding a balance in their work and being able to separate themselves from their typical undergraduate or graduate student role. If they are new to a community or without a strong personal support base on campus, it is difficult to separate work from social life. Since most of us got into the field because we love to work with students, it is often difficult if not impossible to say "no" to student requests for late night, weekend, or even overnight commitments. Staff who develop good rapport with students will undoubtedly be asked to give more and more of their time (there will always be one more thing that needs to be done yesterday)! New professionals will benefit by establishing a work routine that shows that they value their health, their personal and family commitments, and their own sanity, as well as their professional commitment. I have literally had to tell some young staff to take time off so they can get much-needed rest and perspective away from a work problem. If your only friends are those with whom you work, you will never really get away from the work environment. Finding ways to volunteer in your community and establish non-work relationships are healthy alternatives, which can also foster a healthy balance in your life.

McDonald reflects:

Job responsibilities, committee work, personal life, and future planning are all challenges that I have had to learn to balance as a new professional. Finding appropriate boundaries between having recently been a student and now being a professional administrator are difficult. Even more challenging is finding the appropriate balance of involvement and time in the job and my personal life.

My classmates in graduate school came up with "The Top Ten Reasons I Went into Student Affairs." One of them was "the flexible hours - you can work 80 hours a week whenever you want." I knew that expectations would be high for my presence at after-hours events and that some weekends would be devoted to projects, but what I did not comprehend was the true root of the challenge of achieving balance. That is, determining what opportunities are the most important and, when appropriate, how to say "no." As new professionals, we typically have more regular contact with students than directors and often have to plan to adapt to their unique schedules. Being an enthusiastic new professional who is eager to please and learn, I have often been asked to help with committees, workshops, and events both within and outside of my department. These are wonderful opportunities to make connections and develop skills, but if I took every chance to contribute, I am afraid my own job responsibilities would not be met and I would be emotionally and physically drained. I have found that the best supervisors and mentors remind me to take time for myself and establish healthy behaviors that will in turn make me a more effective and efficient professional. Taking time to analyze the potential contributions that I can make with each opportunity and having the support to say no to some things is extremely important.

There is a complex relationship between innovation and tradition that is especially present in a university environment, and finding the balance between the two on the job can be a challenge. Our mission is to establish and apply new knowledge, and yet, we revere century-old traditions and have been criticized for being slow to change. As a brand new professional, I had ideas of how to "mix things up" and had been conditioned to evaluate, assess, and then change everything before evaluating again. At times I was struck with awe that there were certain procedures or policies that had been in place longer than the most senior staff members in my department. How could this be? What I learned was that there were some very good reasons for always doing things a certain way that had been developed over long periods of time before my presence. I have learned not to expect to change everything all at once. I have looked to seasoned professionals for ways to evaluate and to discuss change without the assumptions that it should happen immediately or all at once.

WHAT DO NEW PROFESSIONALS NEED FROM SUPERVISORS AND STUDENT AFFAIRS LEADERSHIP?

New professionals need help in defining their jobs, while looking for new responsibilities and broadening expectations. They must have permission to ask questions and be allowed to make mistakes in building experience and competence. They need assistance in assessing their career path, charting it, and preparing for future steps. Like all professionals, they need systematic feedback, evaluation, and assessment in order to progress in their careers.

McDonald says:

I do not think that I ever asked myself what I needed from my supervisor or my vice president when I started my first position. What I realized after a few months was that I needed mentoring. I needed encouragement to speak up with new ideas, I needed a sounding board to help me make the right decisions, and I needed someone to help me understand the culture and expectations of my new employer. I sought direct feedback from supervisors and inspiration and assurance from my vice president. My supervisor was effective in encouraging me to ask questions about not only my job, but his as well. It was essential for me to understand how to figure out my individual responsibilities and how I fit in with the university environment. This helped to give me an idea of what direction I wanted to take within the profession. My vice president shared her vision of the profession at our institution; she inspired us all to take care of ourselves along with our students as well as to affirm the importance of our efforts. She also provided true leadership for our division when faced with budget cuts and unusual circumstances. She made me feel more secure about my department's future and gave me a sense of pride in being a part of Student Affairs.

New professionals, no matter what their background and education are, need help from student affairs leaders to make sense of their new surroundings, campus culture, professional expectations, and their specific responsibilities. We need to not only be welcomed onto the team, but also mentored to help us make appropriate decisions about continuing to contribute to the team and the profession. We need to be encouraged to ask questions and allowed to make mistakes while building experience and knowledge. This happens through regular and honest feedback from caring professionals who take the time to mentor us. Modeling healthy lifestyles and explaining strategies and goals can inspire us to continue in the field and strive to make our own contributions to the profession now and in the future.

Snyder adds:

Senior student affairs administrators bear the responsibility of setting the professional climate of the division and promoting a culture that enhances bringing new professionals along through support and encouragement. Just as the success of our universities is determined by the accomplishments of our graduates, so too is the success of our student affairs programs and services determined by our staff at all levels, and their ability to be effective in their work and their lives. New professionals should look for those who are open to answering questions and sharing their advice, especially when it is apparent that they are respected members of the college or university community. The core of our profession is service to others and we are marked by our sense of commitment to our students and our colleagues. Those who are self-serving have little future in our work, and new professionals should expect that they will work in an environment that is nurturing and supportive. The adage that one needs to ask for what they want is certainly true, and we are privileged to be in a profession where guidance and help are so readily available. My greatest joy and pride have come from working with young staff, watching them grow and succeed and move on to their own wonderful careers.

CONCLUSION

Welcoming new staff into a student affairs division represents a challenge and an opportunity for senior student affairs administrators. It is a time of excitement and wonder for most new professionals who are eager to get started on a career with an energy that is infectious. Getting started in a positive manner, gaining new experiences, making mistakes and learning from them, and preparing for the future are goals that can be met through mentoring and support, so that new staff and senior administrators learn from one another. This is the nature of our profession— to continue to learn and grow in our work so that the students we serve receive the benefit. With this common goal, we are all destined for success.

CHAPTER 2

Unwritten Rules: Organizational and Political Realities of the Job

MARILYN J. AMEY

Higher education is political. Experienced professionals will recognize the truth in this statement, but for new professionals in student affairs administration, the political nature of the world they recently entered may feel like a cruel joke. They may have studied college administration and perhaps even administrative theory in their graduate programs, but translating textbook examples and theories to real world situations can be challenging. This chapter provides new professionals with some tools with which to assess organizational culture and gives suggestions for successfully managing this culture and its politics. For purposes of this discussion, Kuh and Hall's (1993) definition of culture is used:

> [The] collective, mutually shaping patterns of institutional history, mission, physical settings, norms, traditions, values, practices, beliefs and assumptions which guide behavior of individuals and groups . . . and which provide frames of reference for interpreting the meanings of events and actions on and off campus. (p. 2)

After briefly describing the political nature of today's higher education institutions, I present several common dilemmas facing new administrators, situations that might not conform to their expectations. Each dilemma is, in part, a product or function of the work environment and, as a result, may be ameliorated through a better understanding of organizational culture. Because new professionals are more likely to see themselves as new counselors, programmers, or hall directors than as new administrators, they do not always have a context for understanding and dealing with institutional challenges. Therefore, an approach to organizational analysis is presented and related generally to student affairs work and specifically to the dilemmas confronting new professionals. Answers are not given; the approach to understanding organizational culture is not intended as a panacea. What is suggested is that being an effective organizational analyst, that is, understanding the organizational and political realities of the job, may be key to addressing essential professional issues that are generally not taught in graduate school.

THE ENVIRONMENT OF STUDENT AFFAIRS WORK

Becoming a good organizational analyst, or cultural broker...is key to survival and effective practice in a political organization.

Compared to the corporate and private sectors, educational organizations are often touted as collegial institutions whose members are drawn together by a common mission to serve students and provide an educated citizenry. Lofty goals, rich traditions, ceremonies full of regalia, pomp, and circumstance, and an air of elitism are stereotypical images of colleges and universities, and *family* is an often-used metaphor in describing their atmosphere (Bergquist, 1993; Birnbaum, 1988). In most cases, the vernacular definition of collegial (friendly) may accurately reflect colleges and universities today, but the organizational definition (small in size, shared goals, face-to-face interaction, consensus decision-making, minimized status differentials (Birnbaum, 1988) applies less often. Institutional growth or decline, diversification, technological advancement, entrepreneurial spirit, decentralization, and cultural diversification are just some of the factors that can affect the collegial atmosphere and change the way that the college functions.

Appleton (1991) suggests that while all colleges and universities are political organizations, those that have diffuse goals and are affected by more complex sets of constituencies and organizational patterns are especially susceptible to political behavior. In an era of declining resources, increasing competition for students, and conflicting demands, even small, private, liberal arts colleges, long held up as a model of the non-political or, at least, the less political (Birnbaum, 1988), are becoming arenas for coalition building, "win-lose" games, ambiguous goals, and uneven power distribution. While the idea of politics and political organizations tends to evoke negative connotations, nothing about this approach to decision-making and organizational behavior is inherently negative (Bolman & Deal, 1997). New professionals who are unaware of the nature of organizations or do not understand political functioning, however, can negatively affected quite easily. Becoming a good organizational analyst, or cultural broker, as Stage and Manning (1992) would say, is key to survival and effective practice in a political organization.

At the same time, new professionals also need a clear sense of personal identity in order to avoid being swept away by the institutional gamesmanship that can occur when competition for scarce resources increases positioning and posturing. A strong sense of personal ethics, morality, and integrity serves as an important foundation for effective practice and is the key to organizational leadership (Badaracco & Ellsworth, 1989; Bogue, 1985; Bogue, 1994; see

Chapter 3 in this monograph), yet these factors are not often discussed in graduate degree programs, in new member orientations, or even among trusted colleagues. New practitioners must reconcile their own personal expectations with the professional realities of the organization.

ISSUES OF DISSONANCE CONFRONTING NEW PROFESSIONALS

No matter how carefully we prepare for a job interview, how thoroughly we question those employed at the institution, how confidently we assume the responsibilities of a new job, inevitably, once the newness begins to wear off (and sometimes even sooner), we realize that our expectations do not always match the job's realities. The nature of the administrative position, the college or university where one is employed, and the substance of the gap between expectations and realities vary, of course, from individual to individual. Even so, new student affairs professionals consistently face similar areas of dissonance. While the list could be extended, four broad issues of dissonance frequently appear in the literature on administration—role conflict or ambiguity; lack of systematic evaluation and feedback; professional opportunities or lack thereof; and academic or experiential preparation—issues that can often be addressed or reconciled through a better understanding of organizational culture.

Role Conflict or Ambiguity. New student affairs professionals are often torn by conflicting job demands, differences of opinion with supervisors, or having to do things they do not want to do or are very uncomfortable doing, such as terminating another's employment. The experience of role conflict can be especially severe for those who make the transition directly from senior year in college to the first position in student affairs. Although many entry-level positions today require or prefer a master's degree, many others require only a baccalaureate degree; as a result, the transition sometimes takes place in a matter of days, as one goes from being a student, i.e., one of the group, to being in charge, i.e., a leader. The dissonance caused by role conflicts can be especially overwhelming at this stage, when organizational understanding, influence, and the power to resolve the conflicts are often lacking. One new professional offers an example of this anxiety:

What was most difficult was having to separate from the group of Greek leaders. We thought we had developed such a very strong working relationship with them, everything was going so well. We really thought this was the best group of leaders yet. But while we were at the conference, and they all started drinking right there in front of us . . . We knew they weren't of legal age, and yet they did it right in front us. I'm not sure if they wanted us to do something or not, but we couldn't stay there with them. It would have

15

been like sanctioning their behavior. I just couldn't believe they would put us in that kind of position . . . I thought we all were friends but they crossed the line that night and I don't know how to go back now. [Greek Advisor]

Another aspect of dissonance is role ambiguity, which arises when the new professional is unsure of the scope and responsibilities of the job, job objectives, and colleague expectations (Rasch, Hutchison, & Tollefson, 1986). Positions may seem very clearly defined on paper, but so much of every student affairs administrative position falls under the *other* category of the job description that the true scope of a job seems ever-evolving and, sometimes, never-ending. The expectations of colleagues and supervisors also play a role in defining the scope of a position, depending on the organizational culture. In small colleges, for instance, it may be tacitly understood that administrators are expected to attend various institutional activities regardless of the relationship of the activities to their specific position. At both large and small institutions, involvement in committee work may be an unstated but important element of job responsibilities. As with other elements of culture, these expectations may not be articulated until they have been violated in some way.

It is also true that while organizational charts and position descriptions provide an interpretation of the reality of the job, many basic functions cut across organizational lines and formal reporting structures (Sandeen, 1996). In part because of the inter-related way in which units work together to serve students and in part because of the inherently political nature of educational organizations, new professionals must understand the culture within their own primary work unit and also of the other units with which they work on behalf of students. A sense of dissonance can arise as one straddles different cultural boundaries, where norms, values, behaviors, jargon, and rewards differ.

Lack of Systematic Evaluation and Feedback.

Everything was going fine . . . or so I thought. The students liked me, we were doing some really exciting things, and had come together as a team in a really short time. So you see why I was so shocked to get my six-month evaluation and find out the supervisor didn't want to keep me, that she felt I wasn't "working out." I was very honest about myself when I interviewed; they said I was "just the kind of person they needed!" I never saw it coming . . . [Assistant Activities Director]

In every setting, there are processes or sets of experiences by which newcomers learn the norms, values, and behavioral expectations. During this early period of socialization, issues of role conflict are either lessened or heightened (Louis, 1980), as the new professional tests his or her expectations about the position against the realities of the work environment. If the gap in expectations is too great, the resulting dissonance may lead to the person leaving the position. Feedback, both positive and negative, can be very important during the first few months in closing the expectations gap and relieving dissonance. Most new professionals rely heavily, although not exclusively, on their immediate supervisor for feedback (Coleman & Johnson, 1990). At the same time, colleges and universities are notoriously weak in providing systematic, timely, and constructive feedback to employees. The socialization period may not even include training—or at least sufficient training for new professionals to feel their questions are resolved. Newcomers, especially those who are in their first post-degree professional position, may be unsure of which questions to ask or afraid of appearing too insecure, and so may be particularly reluctant to seek feedback actively and early on, thereby increasing their own sense of stress and transition dissonance. This is often the case for women and people of color who may be underrepresented and, therefore, may feel more at risk.

Professional Opportunities or Lack Thereof. Most people accept a position because they believe opportunities will exist for personal and professional growth. Problems can arise, however, when such opportunities do not materialize. Promotion is often associated with an increase in decision-making authority, control of resources, and opportunities for having an impact on the organization and for making changes. Many associate directors, directors, and deans are actually more constrained by demands on their time, increased responsibilities, increased administrivia, and the structure, values, and norms of their units than it at first appears (Mills, 1993). Those aspects of student affairs work that appeal to many new professionals (i.e., working closely with students, programming) are engaged in less frequently, or at least more narrowly, by senior administrators.

New professionals must reconcile their own personal expectations with the professional realities of the organization.

Horizontal movement is often proposed as an alternative means of enhancing one's job and expanding one's skills prior to moving up in the organization (Young, 1990). Certainly this strategy can be a good choice. At the same time, depending on whether the move occurs within or across divisions, in the same or a different institution, opportunities may vary substantially. Prior comparable experience is not always seen as such, and, as a result, lateral moves may perpetuate a "life at entry level" cycle rather than offer an opportunity to gain broader experience. Finally, opportunity is in large part a result of who is ahead of you on the ladder, as noted by the following new professional:

When I found out I was going to shift over full-time to the Advising Center after having worked there part-time for a year, I was thrilled. They told me my knowledge and expertise were going to be invaluable to the new team and I couldn't wait to get started. What they didn't tell me was that, in the new structure, the Director calls the shots—all of them. I may have expert-

ise but I'm not getting to use it. Most of the time, I'm just supposed to sit there and do what's handed to me . . . Now I'm just looking to move out. [Advising Center Counselor]

As seen in this example, a supervisor unwilling to delegate important responsibilities or share "plum assignments" and committee activities effectively limits the growth, development, and institutional exposure of fellow administrators (Amey, 1991). New professionals must be aware of the impact of the hierarchical and personnel structures of their organization on how they think about themselves, their mobility, and opportunities.

Academic or Experiential Preparation. The higher education/student affairs master's degree provides an orientation to the field and initial employment experiences, often in the form of paid assistantships and for-credit practica. From a review of programs listed in the 1994 ACPA *Directory of Graduate Preparation Programs in College Student Personnel,* it is clear that most entry-level graduate programs provide common academic experiences for their students. The experiential component of degree programs is particularly variable, however, most notably in the extent to which classroom skills and work experiences are mutually transferable. It is not always clear whether the combination of in- and out-of-class experiences adequately prepares new professionals to "hit the ground running" in their first post-degree positions and to succeed in the profession (Ambler, Amey, & Reesor, 1994), a question that is most pressing in the minds of students themselves, as noted by the following new professional:

My classes in the master's program were fine; I learned a lot from my assistantship too—a ton. But it was like living in two different worlds! The faculty hadn't been in practice for a long time, some of them not at all, and the supervisors, well, they just kept saying, "Don't give me theory. This is real life!" I wish we'd had more of an opportunity to bridge the gap. Sometimes it was hard to know which way to go . . . [Recreation Services Director]

Because there is no specific undergraduate academic preparation (i.e., no undergraduate major in student affairs), people enter the field from a wide variety of disciplines. This is obviously true for positions requiring only a baccalaureate degree but also for those positions requiring only a master's degree. Previous work experience is almost as varied as academic major: an admissions recruiter may come from work in the private sector and a financial aid counselor may come with a law degree. The mix is rich. The generalist nature of entry-level student affairs professionals and graduate degree programs serves the institution well in enabling it to attract a multicultural work force. But, for new professionals, this same generalist approach can often lead to insecurity, difficulty in relating to peers, a sense that "others must know more than me," and to feelings of being overwhelmed by all there is to know and learn.

Each of the four dilemmas described above can cause dissonance for new student affairs professionals. At the same time, curbing the confusion, closing the gap between expectations and reality, and learning to deal with the work environment can be accomplished by employing strategies for understanding organizational culture. Since the degree of dissonance created by these dilemmas, and by many others, is a function of the specific institution and unit, the analytic tools presented are generic. The specific solutions reside within each new professional and the individual circumstances of employment and career.

THEORY TO PRACTICE—A CULTURAL FRAMEWORK FOR PROFESSIONAL SURVIVAL

New professionals will not likely find many quick fixes for eliminating the gaps between expectations and realities as they try to survive and thrive in their organizations. At the same time, many issues that hit new professionals head on, such as those described above, seem embedded in the organization itself. One strategy that is often overlooked by new professionals as they transition to the new job is to make an effort to understand organizational culture and become a more effective organizational analyst. As one newer professional stated,

The best course I took while in grad school was [on organizational governance] where we talked about decision-making, and politics, and why things work the way they do, and how to figure it all out. This is what I really needed to know to survive!

In presenting an analytic framework for this chapter, I adapted Tierney's (1991) six essential components of organizational culture: environment, mission, socialization, information, strategy, and leadership. Understanding the dynamics of culture through analysis of these six organizational components can help reduce potential dissonance that results from a gap between the expectations and the organizational and political realities of the job. Being familiar with the values, norms, rituals, symbols, myths, and impact of leadership helps new professionals recognize those behaviors and strategies most likely to succeed (or fail) within their unit. Understanding the culture provides administrators with a means not only for assessing their institutions and departments, but also for identifying tasks and appropriate roles for themselves, thereby reducing some of the dissonance created by role conflict and role ambiguity. As Whitt (1993) suggests, "the potential reward [of discovering the culture of an organization] is greater understanding of both the visible and the tacit elements—the furniture, scripts, and invisible props. . ." (p. 93). Organizational analysis is not a cure for all the difficult times facing new professionals. Other important factors influencing administrative effectiveness and success are: sense making;

awareness of ideologies, rituals, and symbols that motivate and alienate members; identifying key supporters and networks; and re-conceptualizing leadership as an embodiment of these ideals.

Environment. Just as every organization has multiple external and internal environments that have an impact on effectiveness (Bolman & Deal, 1997; Weick, 1991), student affairs divisions operate within many internal environments (e.g., departments within divisions, levels of directors within departments) and external environments. Some are located outside of the specific division but within the same institution, such as academic affairs, business affairs, and athletics. Others are external to the college or university altogether, such as national Greek organizations, the community, private sector suppliers, and the federal government. On a daily basis, not all internal and external environments exert great influence on the work, but, in some ways, these environments shape the context of work and even the daily tasks and assignments of new professionals. New professionals who believe that they only work for their direct supervisor are taking a very shortsighted and narrow perspective. Supervisors help define the environments that are most important, which is helpful, but often new professionals become so engrossed in performing the tasks for which they were hired that they fail to grasp and understand the larger contexts. For example, changes in national accreditation standards in professional degree programs such as business or education might at first seem irrelevant to student affairs work; indeed, many new professionals may even be unaware that accrediting agencies exist. Yet, when looking more closely, those involved with recruitment, scholarships, educational support services, and cultural support services may see changes in their work as they help students adhere to these new (and usually higher) academic standards.

An example much closer to home is the importance of understanding beliefs held about student affairs professionals by non-student affairs units within the college or university, particularly the faculty. At some schools, for a variety of reasons, the professional staff and the faculty work closely together, especially in areas affecting students. Collegial relationships abound, faculty involvement in programming activities is the norm, and co-curricular activities are seen as valuable contributions to the overall growth and development of students (Kuh, Schuh, Whitt, et al., 1991). At other institutions, academic and non-academic units are more separate and even perceived as antagonistic (Komives & Woodard, 1996). Individual interactions may be cooperative, but real collaboration is less likely. The interdependence of units and professionals in serving the student is either less valued or less well understood. In these settings, new professionals are often caught off guard and dismayed to hear their work described as, "taking a load off faculty shoulders," "interfering with students' study time," or "not central to the institutional mission" when budget cuts are being discussed. Becoming an effective environmental scanner, both inside and outside of one's immediate office, helps in understanding which influences matter most and how values and beliefs held by others will have an impact on the daily activities of the new professional. Such scanning is a key element to succeeding in an institution.

Mission. At some point or another, every new professional comes in contact with a student handbook or a piece of recruitment material that contains the institution's mission statement. Usually a lengthy and lofty text, the mission statement supposedly describes what an institution does, how and for whom, and sometimes even provides a discussion of the social, ethical, and educational beliefs that shape the institutional context (Lyons, 1993). Divisions of student affairs often have their own mission statements that reflect the larger institutional mission but also describe more specifically the work of the division in relation to students; individual units within a division may have their own versions as well. As guiding texts, these various mission statements provide a loose framework for organizing daily activities; as cultural artifacts, they often do not explain what really happens in the lives of new professionals. This is especially true in academic organizations, known for their multiple and competing missions.

Kuh and Schuh suggest, "The 'living mission' of a college is how students, faculty, administrators, graduates, and others describe what the college is and is trying to accomplish" (1991, p. 12). These descriptions of purpose help the new professional understand more fully what the practice of student affairs means in each institutional context. Looking for areas of both agreement and disagreement in others' depictions of the office's mission gives a clearer sense of what the office really is about, for whom and how it will work. New professionals can find descriptions of purpose in a vice president for student affairs' comments at the fall semester division gathering, in a director's design of professional training, in the criteria presented for staff evaluation, and in day-to-day talk around the office. The messages may not be the same. Greatest agreement may exist at smaller, private liberal arts colleges where frequent interactions among faculty and staff reinforce a set of beliefs, values, and traditions (reflecting a stronger organizational culture) while the greatest disparity may occur at the large research university where multiple sets of beliefs, values, and traditions likely exist. Institutional and, therefore, student affairs units' missions can also be affected by history and heritage, organizational type and complexity of purpose, and type of student served.

Finding consistent messages is only part of the assessment; recognizing places where mission and belief statements conflict is also critical to success as a new professional. When the espoused mission, i.e. what we say, diverts from the mission in use, i.e., what we do (adapted from Argyris & Schon, 1977), the new professional may find that a lack of agreement about the goals of the unit exists, that a sense of common purpose does not drive or shape decisions, that there is less than strong support for work done within the unit by those external to it, and that a clash has developed between institutional or unit activity, or both, and one's own value system. Remembering that the mission exists both on paper and in the minds and actions of members should lead to a different kind of questioning during the interview process and a greater awareness of the culture during the early socialization period when new administrators are often preoccupied with learning specific tasks and buoyed by the euphoria of a new job.

Socialization. All organizations engage in rituals and ceremonies for the welcoming of new members. These activities may be as limited as having newcomers complete the perfunctory employment forms and purchase a parking permit or as extensive as having them attend orientation programs and staff retreats. In the same way that we think of orienting students to campus or initiating inductees into student organizations, student affairs units *bring new members into the fold* through planned activities and help create a sense of shared meaning about the work, the unit, the members of the unit, and the larger college or university. In addition to providing an idea of who's who and what's what, socialization, as Tierney (1991) describes it, is a process of becoming aware of and indoctrinated to the norms, beliefs, and values of the organization. This socialization process is related less to administrative functions than to the development of social consciousness, less concerned with short-term job tasks than with long-term direction and purpose. As the new professional begins to develop an identity as a member of a department and to gain a sense of self within the larger student affairs profession, socialization often plays a key role in providing knowledge of what is required to succeed and to excel.

One thing that affects both early and ongoing socialization is the professional anchoring of an individual's position to the department and the institution. Professional anchoring refers to the primary orientation and interaction patterns of a position. For example, does the position demand that one work most often with employees in the same office or unit (internal) or with those in other offices outside the unit (external)? In many ways, it can be argued that student affairs as a division embraces a very interactive, externally oriented set of positions because members work with so many non-student affairs people to get the job done. New professionals in advising or educational support services, for example, quickly come to understand the importance of building close relationships with faculty departments as well as with admissions and student orientation staffs (Amey, 1991). Such an external focus keeps the new professional aware of the larger college or university, its culture, and its method of functioning, because attention is not primarily directed within the unit.

At the same time, many student affairs positions seem very internally focused on a daily basis, either within the office or program itself or on students, rather than on interactions with other non-student employees. Such positions tend to be fairly self-contained and emphasize more depth than breadth in professional growth. Advanced positions within student housing and financial aid, for example, may require specialization and, therefore, will not encourage the same range of increased broad institutional knowledge. Individuals in more internally anchored positions may have to create their own opportunities, apart from job responsibilities, for developing relationships and interacting with the broader college community. The networks and support systems one develops can help with this, especially as the increased use of technology makes inter- and intra-institutional connecting easier. Institutional volunteerism, such as committee work, is another excellent way to stay connected outside the office (see Chapters 6 and 8 of this monograph).

Information. Tierney's (1991) fourth essential component of organizational culture is information. In assessing the organizational and political realities, an early task of new professionals is to determine what constitutes information, who has it, and how it is disseminated. Even in a highly structured organization, where memos, written records, handbooks, and standard operating procedures abound (Birnbaum, 1988), information does not only flow hierarchically, from the top down. Certainly this is the case as one moves into organizations characterized as more collegial or political (Birnbaum, 1988; Bolman & Deal, 1997). Listservs, on-line resources, and e-mail communication enhances the speed and volume of information flow, often making accessible instantly that which traditionally had to be provided by an information gatekeeper. At the same time, communication explosion does not always mean information accuracy. New professionals must become skilled at gathering information from multiple sources and in multiple forms. Waiting for "official word" may mean missing an opportunity or not being able to avoid a crisis. In such situations, the relationships that have been developed with key colleagues can be critical to getting the job done effectively and efficiently. Knowing whom to call for the "right" answer is not always a function of a person's position on the organizational chart.

New professionals also become quickly aware of the numerous points of view that exist in every college or university. Gathering information from multiple sources allows for a kind of triangulation, where one can draw conclusions based on areas of agreement among sources (Patton, 1990). This can be critical in curbing rumors, creating coalitions, and seizing creative opportunities. Informal networks also provide important information, serving as critical sounding boards for ideas and as ways of gathering feedback for professional growth and development. Learning with whom one can work closely and developing those relationships is not often a conscious activity, though research on academic leaders suggests it should be more intentional (Winship, 1991). As one new professional explained,

Rich and I have a standing lunch the third Thursday of every month. He's been here two years longer than me, and works in [another unit], so I'm always looking to him for advice, to figure out what's really going on. He's been great to talk with, and introduces me to lots of folks he knows. [Hall Director]

Strategy. Many new professionals believe that most decisions are straightforward, that the designated leader has the final say-so, and that their own authority is very limited. Others sought or were hired into an institution that touted a team or participative approach to management, where everyone would be involved in decisions and discussions of mission, goal setting, and evaluation. Still others believed they were being hired into one of the two approaches described above but found the reality to be very different. It is important to recognize the difference between talk and action, between espoused theory and theory in use related to decision-making (Argyris & Schon, 1977) and to become aware of the way things get done as quickly as possible. All of these aspects reflect what Tierney (1991) calls "organizational strategy." Strategy, as a component of culture, is often overlooked because of its perceived complexity, yet it is a central feature in navigating the organizational waters.

Becoming familiar with both the obvious and the subtle ways in which decisions are made—who is involved and at what level, and what the penalties are for ineffective decisions and the rewards for effective ones—is part of understanding your unit. Unfortunately, these things are often learned by trial and error and by observing rather than by questioning others. New professionals can begin gathering information about the strategies used within their own office early in the socialization period by asking some basic questions. Is this the kind of unit where the director signs off on everything before you are allowed to move ahead? Are symbols and symbolic meaning (including something as simple as event T-shirts) prevalent and effectively used throughout the office? At department meetings, is everything discussed, from what to give the secretary on his birthday to next year's budget proposal? If the supervisor casually mentions an upcoming event, do you really have a choice to attend? Does an invitation to be creative and innovative and to take the lead mean only within tacit limits? A clear sense of proper procedures, cliques, active counter-cultures, and the informal networks that abound in every organization helps a new professional work more effectively and efficiently, build supportive connections, capitalize on opportunities, and succeed more consistently on behalf of students.

Leadership. Organizational charts show those in positional authority, the formal leaders of the unit (even though "leader" may be a misnomer in terms of their actual behaviors). One must pay attention to the organizational culture to discern those whose title (or lack thereof) and position belie their role as leader—the informal leaders of the college or university. New professionals willingly accept the leader status of those in positions of authority, but it is often the informal leaders who wield more power and influence over daily activities in student affairs. A long-standing mid-level director may not appear to be as strong a leader as her senior level supervisor if one judges only by title and position, but her institutional knowledge and well-established reputation as a team player may allow her to exercise significant leadership throughout the division. Another person may live (or work) next door to the college president and so is often able to raise important issues and concerns without an appointment, even though he holds an "assistant to" position, which is often seen by administrative theorists as indicating low status (Moore, Salimbene, Marlier, & Bragg, 1983). Good practice, organizational intuition, and a willingness to get involved are often key elements of informal leadership, more so than title and place on the organizational chart.

People who are motivated to choose careers in student affairs tend to look early on for ways to develop and exercise their own leadership. If a culture of leadership exists at the institution, then members throughout the organization engage in ongoing professional development and organizational learning (Senge, 1998). Senge suggests that real leaders, who may or may not hold positions of formal authority, are open learners themselves who inspire in others the confidence and will to work collectively to create new answers and identify new issues (Lewis, 1994; Senge, 1990,1998). In many ways, this is similar to the learning imperative to which we subscribe in working with students. If Senge and others are right, one's place in the formal organizational hierarchy is less important than one's exercise of personal leadership; this can be an important lesson for new professionals to remember.

I never saw myself as a leader before—that really sounded so "out there" to me. I'm a helper, and I guess being the leader always seemed less important. And then I sat on two committees, and there were things to be done, so of course I just jumped in to help get the work done and all of a sudden everyone is calling me the leader, looking to me for leadership. It was weird! I guess that's what I was doing, but I also kept saying to myself, "Who am I? I don't have that fancy office or a long title." No one seemed to be worried about that but me. . . [Multicultural Affairs Counselor]

As this practitioner learned, there is a close connection between effective leaders and effective followers. Much of what is written focuses only on the leadership side of the equation. The bookshelves of senior administrators are

> A clear sense of proper procedures, cliques, active counter-cultures, and the informal networks that abound in every organization helps a new professional work more effectively and efficiently...

full of works by leadership strategists promoting seven steps or five keys or eight things to remember. While these books have their place, the work of those who promote effective followers (De Pree, 1993; Kelley, 1998; Lee, 1993), team leadership (Bensimon & Neumann, 1993; Heider, 1989), and servant leaders (Bogue, 1994; Pollard, 1996) are equally important and perhaps more vital to the multicultural higher education institution of the future. In addition, because the face of leadership within student affairs itself is changing slowly, it is important for new professionals to see themselves in leadership roles where role models may not yet exist. Blackmore (1989), Cross and Revekas (1990), Curry, (2000), and Ideta (1996) are only a few of the writers presenting different lenses for examining (and finding!) leadership that departs from traditionally perpetuated images and narrow bands of acceptable behavior (Morrison, 1993). Whether through readings, conference participation, networking, or insightful supervisors and role models, new professionals should consciously strive for opportunities to engage in leadership/followership development and begin to see themselves as potential leaders in their organizations and in the student affairs profession.

CONCLUSION

Many of the dilemmas facing new professionals present difficult challenges not easily resolved through cookbook philosophies or "how-to" lists. Becoming an effective organizational analyst changes the nature of questions asked during job interviews, perhaps leading to a better initial institutional fit. It also presents a different way of interacting with the college or university, the student affairs unit, its members, and even the job itself.

New professionals are busy learning the specific tasks required of their position, making personal transitions, and going through numerous balancing adjustments during the first few months on the job, many of which are addressed in subsequent chapters of this monograph. At the same time, if new professionals take an organizational, analytic approach to their own professional transition, such as Tierney's (1991) framework described in this chapter, they will think about issues such as: What are the important units with which I will interact? What are the agreed upon values and beliefs of my unit and where is there disagreement? How will I get connected within and apart from my office? Who are the key people to know and why? Where will my support systems be? How do decisions get made and by whom? And who are the informal leaders as well as those in positions of authority? Using this approach encourages new professionals to ask different questions and attend to different aspects of their work environment, especially during, but certainly not limited to, the first few months on the job, during the socialization period when gaps between expectations and job realities can most easily be addressed.

REFERENCES

Ambler, D. A., Amey, M. J., & Reesor, L. M. (1994, March). *Strategies for improving collaboration between faculty and practitioners.* Paper presented at the meeting of the National Association for Student Personnel Association, Dallas, TX.

American College Personnel Association. (1994). *Directory of graduate preparation programs in college student personnel, 1994.* Washington, DC: Author.

Amey, M. J. (1991). Bridging the gap between expectations and reality. In K. M. Moore & S. B. Twombly (Eds.), *Administrative careers and the marketplace* (New Directions for Higher Education, No. 72, pp. 78-88). San Francisco: Jossey-Bass.

Appleton, J. (1991). The context. In P. L. Moore (Ed.), *Managing the political dimension of students affairs* (New Directions for Student Services, No. 55, pp. 5-17). San Francisco: Jossey-Bass.

Argyris, C., & Schon, D. A. (1977). *Organizational learning: A theory of action perspective.* Reading, MA: Addison-Wesley.

Badaracco, J. L., & Ellsworth, R. R. (1989). *Leadership and the quest for integrity.* Boston: Harvard Business School Press.

Bensimon, E. M., & Neumann, A. (1993). *Redesigning collegiate leadership: Teams and teamwork in higher education.* Baltimore: The Johns Hopkins Press.

Bergquist, W. H. (1993). *The four cultures of the academy.* San Francisco: Jossey-Bass.

Birnbaum, R. (1988). *How colleges work.* San Francisco: Jossey-Bass.

Blackmore, J. (1989). Educational leadership: A feminist critique and reconstruction. In J. Smyth (Ed.), *Critical perspectives on educational leadership* (pp. 93-130). NY: The Falmer Press.

Bogue, E. G. (1985). *The enemies of leadership: Lessons for leaders in education.* Bloomington, IN: Phi Delta Kappa Educational Foundation.

Bogue, E. G. (1994). *Leadership by design.* San Francisco: Jossey-Bass.

Bolman, L. G., & Deal, T. E. (1997). *Reframing organizations: Artistry, choice, and leadership.* 2nd Edition. San Francisco: Jossey-Bass.

Cross, C., & Revekas, J. E. (1990). Leadership in a different voice. *AAWCJC Journal,* 7-14.

27

Curry, B. (2000). *Women in power: Pathways to leadership in education*. New York: Teachers College Press.

De Pree, M. (1993). Followership. W. E. Rosenbach & R. L. Taylor (Eds.), *Contemporary issues in leadership* (3rd ed., pp. 137-140). Boulder: Westview Press.

Heider, R. (1989). The leader who knows how things happen. In W. E. Rosenbach & R. L. Taylor (Eds.), *Contemporary issues in leadership* (2nd ed., pp. 161-167). Boulder: Westview Press.

Kelley, R. E. (1998). In praise of followers. In Rosenbach, W.E. & Taylor, R. L. (Eds.), *Contemporary Issues in Leadership* (4th ed., pp. 96-106). Boulder: Westview Press.

Ideta, L. M. (1996). *Asian women leaders of higher education: Inclusionary empowerment in pursuit of excellence*. Paper presented at the meeting of the Association for the Study of Higher Education, Memphis, TN.

Komives, S. R., & Woodard, D. B. Jr. (1996). Building on the past, shaping the future. In S. R. Komives, D. B. Woodard, Jr., & Associates (Eds.), *Student services: A handbook for the profession* (3rd ed., pp. 536-555). San Francisco: Jossey-Bass.

Kuh, G. D., & Hall, J. E. (1993). Clinical perspectives in student affairs. In G. D. Kuh (Ed.), *Cultural perspectives in clinical affairs work* (pp. 1-20). Lanham, MD: American College Personnel Association / University Press of America.

Kuh, G. D., & Schuh, J. (1991). *The role and contribution of student affairs in involving colleges*. Washington, DC: National Association of Student Personnel Administrators.

Kuh, G. D., Schuh, J. H., Whitt. E. J., & Associates. (1991). *Involving colleges: Successful approaches to fostering student learning and development outside the classroom*. San Francisco: Jossey-Bass.

Lee, C. (1993). Followership: The essence of leadership. In W. E. Rosenbach & R. L. Taylor (Eds.), *Contemporary Issues in Leadership* (3rd ed., pp. 113-121). Boulder: Westview Press.

Lewis, P. H. (1994). Implementing the culture of leadership. In McDade, S. A. & Lewis, P. H. (Eds.), *Developing administrative excellence: Creating a culture of leadership* (New Directions for Higher Education, No. 87, pp. 93-100). San Francisco: Jossey-Bass.

Louis, M. (1980). Surprise and sense making: What newcomers experience entering unfamiliar organizational settings. *Administrative Science Quarterly, 25*, 226-251.

Lyons, J. W. (1993). The importance of institutional mission. In M.J . Barr & Associates (Eds.), *The handbook of student affairs administration* (pp. 3-15). San Francisco: Jossey-Bass.

Mills, D. B. (1993). The role of the middle manager. In M. J. Barr & Associates (Eds.), *The handbook of student affairs administration* (pp. 121-134). San Francisco: Jossey-Bass.

Moore, K. M., Salimbene, A., Marlier, J., & Bragg, S. (1983). The structure of presidents' and deans' careers. *Journal of Higher Education* 54, 501-515.

Morrison, A. M. (1993). Leadership diversity and leadership challenge. In W. E. Rosenbach & R. L. Taylor (Eds.), *Contemporary issues in leadership* (3rd ed., pp. 159-166). Boulder: Westview.

Pollard, C. W. (1996). The leader who serves. In The Drucker Foundation (Ed.), *The leaders of the future* (pp. 241-248). San Francisco: Jossey-Bass.

Patton, M. (1990). *Qualitative evaluation and research methods* (2nd ed.). Newbury Park, CA: Sage.

Rasch, C., Hutchison, J., & Tollefson, N. (1986). Sources of stress among administrators at research universities. *Review of Higher Education* 9, 419-434.

Sandeen, A. (1996). Organization, functions, and standards of practice. In S. R. Komives, D. B. Woodard, Jr., & Associates (Eds.), *Student services: A handbook for the profession* (3rd ed., pp. 435-457). San Francisco: Jossey-Bass.

Senge, P. M. (1990). *The fifth discipline: The art and practice of the learning organization*. NY: Doubleday.

Senge, P. (1998). Leading learning organizations. In W.E. Rosenbach and R.L. Taylor (eds.), *Contemporary Issues in Leadership*. (4th Edition. p. 174-178.) Boulder: Westview Press.

Stage, F. K. & Manning, K. (1992). *Enhancing the multicultural campus environment: A cultural brokering approach* (New Directions for Student Services, No. 60). San Francisco: Jossey-Bass.

Tierney, W. G. (1991). Organizational culture in higher education: Defining the essentials. In M. Peterson (Ed.), *ASHE reader in organization and governance in higher education* (pp. 126-139). Lexington, MA: Ginn Press.

Weick, K. E. (1991). Educational organizations as loosely coupled systems. In M. Peterson (Ed.), *ASHE reader in organization and governance in higher education* (pp. 103-117). Lexington, MA: Ginn Press.

Whitt, E. J. (1993). "Making the familiar strange": Discovering culture. In G. D. Kuh (Ed.), *Cultural perspectives in clinical affairs work* (pp. 81-94). Lanham, MD: American College Personnel Association / University Press of America.

Winship, S. (1991). *An analysis of gender differences in position paths of community college presidents.* (Unpublished doctoral dissertation, University of Kansas, Lawrence, 1991). Dissertation Abstracts International, 54, A0056.

Young, R. B. (Ed.) (1990). *The invisible leaders: Student affairs mid-managers.* Washington, DC: National Association of Student Personnel Administrators.

Toward an Ethic for the Profession

THOMAS E. MCWHERTOR AND DAVID S. GUTHRIE

INTRODUCTION

Higher education sage Clark Kerr (1994) writes that:

> ...ethics will not go away . . . On campus, students have been raising more ethical questions, particularly since the 1960s, and this has forced administrators and boards of trustees to give them greater attention. This has made campus governance more difficult, since issues of ethical conduct are not subject to easy agreement . . . It can even be said, without too much exaggeration, that higher education is in a crisis of ethics. (p. 147)

Many, if not most educators in America's colleges and universities—including student affairs professionals—quickly agree with Kerr's appraisal. Perhaps more often than not, what is right seems elusive among various stakeholders' contentions that their respective viewpoints on an issue are most important or valid. Likewise, balancing competing interests in making decisions and identifying appropriate courses of action may seem unattainable and perhaps may make effective decision-making impossible.

In this chapter, we want to foster a dialogue about how this so-called "crisis of ethics" might be addressed. We include several "voices" of new professionals at various points throughout the chapter as a means of noting that fascinating, challenging dialogues are currently occurring on this subject.

Although we will refer to ethics per se, we are more concerned about an ethic for the profession. That is, new professionals need to consider the implicit values that give form and nuance to their behaviors and actions. These values emerge within four particular contexts: personal, institutional, professional, and legal. In turn, these contexts provide the situations in which the particular principles of one's ethic are framed and where one's ethics are displayed. By emphasizing both contexts and principles, we hope to offer new professionals a foundation upon which to base more effective ethical decision-making.

A Conceptual Framework for a Professional Ethic and Ethics

Ethics is a word used easily and often in everyday speech. Given this familiarity, one may even assume that substantial agreement exists regarding its meaning and, at a certain level, this assumption may be accurate. That is, many may equate ethics with principled behavior, particular personal characteristics, the essence of responsibility, or appropriate or "right" actions, and they would not be wrong in doing so. At another level, however, we are all aware that people's ethics vary. One person may cherish honesty at all costs while another considers a "harmless" fib ethically appropriate behavior.

Beyond how people may define and practice ethics, we sense that considerably less awareness exists regarding the nature of an ethic. Whether due to a reluctance of the individual to divulge a reason for engaging in a certain action, a lack of self-reflection regarding underlying values, a lack of time always to consider what may lie behind specific actions, or some other issue, conversations about one's ethic seem comparatively rare. Simply deciding what we should do often outweighs any efforts to consider why we should decide to do what we do.

What may be most helpful to new professionals is an exploration of the contours of an individual's ethic as it is expressed in his or her ethics. Acknowledging that ethics may vary given various circumstances, a possible framework in which to make sense of ethical behavior within the profession is presented. In this chapter, we offer: a) an overview of the contexts in which a new professional's ethic is shaped and exists; and b) several fundamental principles and related guidelines that are crucial to a new professional's ethic and provide bridges to ethical behaviors that we believe should characterize professional practice.

The Contexts of a Professional Ethic

The new professional's ethic is expressed whether he or she is discussing a marriage problem (personal), a committee report (institutional), a disciplinary hearing (professional), or a hiring procedure (legal) ...

The appropriate place to begin is with a succinct definition of an ethic. We use *ethic* to refer to the ultimate values or principles that one holds. *Ethic* is a derivative of the Greek word *ethos*, which denotes the essence of one's character. As such, a person's ethic is a reference to those fundamental persuasions that define an individual's character, a description of the self at the core. Moreover, a person's ethic is the wellspring of his or her actions, decisions, and behaviors and is expressed in his or her ethics, at least ideally and most of the time. Someone may, however, as Dalton (1993, p. 90) warns, "say and not do." For example, a dean of students may espouse an ethic of integrity but act with malice in dealing with a personnel matter.

We believe that four interrelated contexts contribute to the development of a new professional's ethic: a) personal; b) institutional; c) professional; and d) legal. These contexts contribute to the shaping of an ethic from which a new professional "does ethics" in responding to and resolving the day-to-day situations and dilemmas that are present within these very same contexts. These contexts not only shape the ethic or values of new professionals but serve as the arenas in which their ethic and ethics are expressed. Each context is elaborated more fully below.

The Personal Context. A new professional's ultimate values—his or her ethic—are clearly shaped by personal characteristics and experiences. Family history, ethnicity, personality traits, gender, religious commitments, race, socioeconomic background, individual accomplishments, academic performance, and physical characteristics—among other factors—shape ultimate values and commitments. Further, these personal characteristics are more than simple demographic descriptors. That is, considerable meaning lies behind being a 21st Century middle-class consumer, a college graduate, a male, an Italian American citizen, and a nominal Methodist, whether or not one intentionally attaches meaning to these terms. These meanings emerge from both past and present settings as individuals, groups, communities, and nations live out their values and commitments. Being unaware of the current and historic meanings that accompany personal characteristics does not enable one to transcend their influence.

In sum, new professionals do not arrive at their institutions unformed, *tabula rasa*, nor do they live within the profession as if other aspects of life do not exist or never existed. Rather, they bring certain values to their jobs and to the profession that have been forged through life circumstances and experiences. The following reflections from a student affairs administrator at a state university illustrate this idea:

I have a colleague who I began to train as a hearing officer in the university judicial system. He was a new professional who had done a good job in other areas of student affairs, so I hoped to "expand" his professional experience by having him learn judicial processes. I explained the educational philosophy of our system, had him observe me in a hearing process, and then asked him to handle a few cases while I observed him. I discovered pretty quickly that he was ineffective in handling this new responsibility. Many violations that occur on our campus are alcohol related. Since he was an avid drinker himself—during his own college days as well as currently—he was unable to sanction students properly because of his own feelings and experiences with alcohol.

New professionals who acknowledge and seek to make sense of the assorted components of personal context heighten their ability to perform effectively in and out of the profession. In contrast, new professionals who devalue the personal context by eschewing self-knowledge, practicing self-deception, or projecting personal problems onto others significantly limit their efforts to facilitate learning among students and to serve others both on and off the job.

Given this potential impact, it is surprising that many of the prime sources on ethics in the student affairs profession (National Association of Student Personnel Administrators, 1990; Winston & McCaffrey, 1983; Winston & Saunders, 1991) either downplay or ignore altogether what we consider an integral component of the discussion, namely an individual's personal values. New professionals would do well to examine the ways in which their own life circumstances and commitments shaped and continue to shape their essential values and the ongoing expression of these values in institutional, professional, and social arenas. Equally important, new professionals may find it helpful to consider more consciously the relationship and symmetry of their personal contexts to other contexts, particularly to the institutional and professional contexts of their ethic.

The Institutional Context. Although the personal context of an individual's ethic is most often overlooked in the canons of student affairs ethics, the role that an institution plays in shaping an ethic also is frequently downplayed in the discussion. The Standards of Professional Practice of the National Association of Student Personnel Administrators (Winston, Anchors, & Associates, 1993, p. 600) urges professionals to "Agree[ment] with Institutional Mission and Goals;" similarly, the American College Personnel Association (Winston, Jr., et al., p. 596) considers "Responsibility to the Institution" one of four essential ethical standards for student affairs professionals. Though the section concerning the institutional context is a brief one in these documents, the sentiment expressed is important. It is imperative to consider the impact of institutional context on the ethic and ethics of new and experienced professionals. Student affairs professionals do not exist in a vacuum. Rather, they work within larger institutional arenas that include particular histories, organizational structures and protocols, overarching missions, internal and external politics, embedded legacies, and the like. Moreover, student affairs professionals do not work independent of the fundamental purpose of the college experience—student learning—or from the other institutional constituencies that are connected to the learning enterprise. Consequently, it is essential that new professionals account for and seek to understand "where they are" institutionally. What may be an ethically acceptable approach at one institution may be grounds for dismissal at another; it is wrongheaded to assume that what works at one college will work at all colleges. A new professional from a public institution in the South sheds life on the relative impact of institutional context:

Our student programming board sponsored a lecture series and one of the lectures was planned to explore the issue of tolerance. The topic was meant to encourage students to be fair to all individuals regardless of personal dif-

ferences. The speaker selected to give the address was a former National League baseball official who had been fired when it became public that he was gay. The lecture created a stir among students, community members, campus religious organizations, and at least one Board member not because of the speaker's perspective on fair labor policies but because he was gay. Although the institution where I work is a four-year public university, it is located in the Bible Belt in the deep South. I have come to understand that many programs that would be acceptable at many public universities are not acceptable here.

This example testifies clearly to the importance of identifying and understanding the formal and informal policies that comprise an institution's culture. Examining how these policies have been and are being interpreted is equally important. Colleagues within the institution or colleagues at similar institutions are often good resources for this valuable information. In the final analysis, new professionals must strive to understand the institutional contexts in which they exist, as well as the ways these contexts correspond to the personal, professional, and legal dimensions of their ethic.

The Professional Context. We now turn to the particular context of an individual's ethic that receives the most attention by far in the student affairs literature. As noted, our sense is that the personal and institutional dimensions of an individual's ethic have been minimized in favor of emphasizing what appropriately may be called the professionalization of professional ethics. Notwithstanding this concern, we acknowledge the importance of the professional context. New professionals have chosen a vocation in which much information is available and many guidelines exist regarding the anticipated values and behaviors that accompany membership (Council for the Advancement of Standards, 1986). Clearly, new professionals should not overlook these signposts of professional integrity. Whether one consults Young's (1993) "essential values," Winston's and McCaffrey's (1983) or Winston's and Saunders' (1991) ethical values and decision-making models, Canon's (1989) ethical standards, or the National Association of Student Personnel Administrators' (1990) or American College Personnel Association's (1989) "standards" (all of which have considerable overlap), the point is that the profession calls on its members to embrace fundamental values in implementing their work. Being a new professional includes acknowledging, if not striving to adhere to, the guidelines of the profession. Moreover, as Dalton (1993) suggests, new professionals do well not only to incorporate these professional values and behaviors personally, but to transmit and promote them among student, faculty, and staff colleagues as well. Only such intentional efforts will, over time, produce an environment conducive to effective ethical decision-making (Canon, 1993).

Professional values are transmitted not only by written statements, but they are passed on among professionals interpersonally as well. In this regard, professional networks are crucial in developing one's framework of knowledge and in holding one accountable to act responsibly with students and peers. New professionals need to establish networks of colleagues with whom they can confer, from whom they can learn, and to whom they can be accountable in everyday decision-making as a hedge against the myopia that comes from working independently within an institution and the errors in judgment that inevitably occur when one works in isolation.

Trusted collegial networks become increasingly important in times when new issues enter the field, such as the growth of information technology over the last decade. New professionals have seen a whole new set of issues introduced into the student affairs field, with the growing dominance of the World Wide Web and electronic communication and publication media—and it is certain that there will be more such issues in the years ahead. Policies developed for other media are being applied to these matters, but entirely new issues have arisen as well. Ethical job performance requires that we rely on other professionals to help navigate new challenges such as these; the professional dimension of one's ethic does not include autonomy. Balancing the professional context of ethic and ethics with the other contexts of one's life requires constant attention and may, at times, become a source of mild dissonance or blatant conflict. However, collegial networks can assist the young professional to resolve these tensions more effectively.

The Legal Context. The legal context of an individual's ethic also receives considerable attention in student affairs literature. Due at least in part to the profession's increasingly close involvement with students' rights issues as well as an ever-more litigious culture, considering the impact of legal issues in the formation of a new professional's ethic is unavoidable. Colleges and universities are significantly affected by what Bellah and associates (1992, p. 80) refer to as the "administered society," in which national, state, and local laws, regulations, and ordinances affect every area of life. Given the increasing range and nuance of issues within the student affairs profession, it is vitally important for new professionals to be current in legal matters. Developing expertise in knowing when an issue does and does not have legal ramifications is essential, especially given the seeming ease with which affronted students currently appeal to the "l-word" (lawsuit). Moreover, gaining experience in clarifying the relationships, if any, between legal considerations and the other contexts mentioned above is a worthy goal.

In summary, we suggest that a new professional's ethic has been shaped and continues to be shaped by personal, institutional, professional, and legal contexts. In turn, one's ethic—affected as it is within these contexts—gives support and meaning to the ethics that a new professional enacts as he or she understands and responds to the issues and problems that arise "at the office." Taking time to evaluate the contexts that have shaped one's ethic and subsequently inform one's ethics is vital to effective leadership in the profession.

Two additional comments are relevant before moving on. First, a new professional's ethic is expressed within the entire range of relationships, including professional associations. That is, a new professional's ethic is not simply a personal matter that is expressed in personal contexts alone but rather operates among each of the contexts mentioned above, with others who have membership within these contexts. The new professional's ethic is manifest in his or her on-the-job relationships with supervisors, subordinates, students, colleagues, parents, and external stakeholders, among others. The new professional's ethic is expressed whether he or she is discussing a marriage problem (personal), a committee report (institutional), a disciplinary hearing (professional), or a hiring procedure (legal) with a student, supervisor, or peer.

Second, a new professional's ethic is not static. Although linking an ethic with ultimate values may conjure up impressions of longevity and uniformity, we suggest that an individual's ethic is always being refined. As new professionals exist within personal, institutional, professional, and legal contexts, they experience glories and glitches in each that continuously modify their ethic. Likewise, the people with whom a new professional co-exists—regardless of the context(s) of these relationships—offer significant contributions to the ongoing development of a personal ethic. In short, a new professional's ethic shapes and is shaped by his or her ethics, including the contexts and relationships in which both an ethic and ethics occur.

CRUCIAL PRINCIPLES FOR A NEW PROFESSIONAL'S ETHIC

Thus far we have defined an ethic and emphasized four contexts that both shape it and function as the arenas in which it is manifested. We also have noted that these contexts are interconnected and that a new professional's ethic is always in process, changing as contexts and persons with whom one interacts change. In this section, we offer three principles that we believe lie at the heart of an ethic for student affairs professionals: a) be informed; b) maintain integrity; and c) practice justice. We share Winston's and Saunders' (1991) concern for "normative ethics" (p. 331). Those familiar with other sources on ethical practices in the student affairs profession will note a similarity between our stated principles and others, and perhaps this is as it should be. For example, Rickard (1993) offers truth, freedom, and justice as the three essential values of the profession. Despite apparent similarities, we also attempt to add certain nuances to the three principles. In the end, our hope is that new professionals will embrace these principles regardless of context and company, at and away from work, now and into the future.

> [T]hree principles ... lie at the heart of an ethic for student affairs professionals: a) be informed; b) maintain integrity; and c) practice justice.

Be Informed. Over 400 years ago, Francis Bacon stated: "Knowledge is power." Indeed, a knowledge base is essential to any field, including student affairs. As noted above, successful new professionals must have foundational understandings of the personal, institutional, professional, and legal contexts within which they operate in order to accomplish given tasks. Typically, higher education in student affairs emphasizes the professional and legal requisites for one's work. It prepares us to know what we need to know and gives us the skills to get that information. In addition, the available literature offers guidelines and principles related to these contexts. Such resources must be consulted regularly, and staying abreast of professional and legal developments is a clearly acknowledged part of the job. Today, this is easier than in the past, with easy access to resources on-line, the opportunity to participate in ongoing electronic discussion groups, and to receive e-mail notices of current issues and changes in professional or legal standards. The young professional must sort through this information and discern which areas are most important to daily responsibilities, since it is impossible to stay on top of everything; one simply must choose the areas in which to stay current.

However, it is not enough simply to stay in touch with the professional and legal aspects of knowledge. Overlooking the following two areas, which are often given short treatment in the literature, limits important aspects of being informed:

1. *Self-knowledge* is a lens through which people understand their work, other people, and the world. As a result, it is incumbent that new professionals evaluate their strengths and weaknesses, their commitments and biases, since these affect the ways they understand their daily tasks and relationships with students and peers. A new professional at a church-related college on the west coast understands the importance of self-knowledge, as indicated by his remarks:

> *My best performance must begin with a willingness to be self-honest and an accurate understanding of personal values before such characteristics and beliefs can be communicated and modeled to others or to my institution. What I believe to be true (about self, others, life, love, the pursuit of happiness, and so on) and why I believe what I believe to be true must be clear to me personally before I can perform with integrity within the context of the profession or my institution.*

Self-knowledge is the root of a new professional's success and, therefore, it should be explored and developed regularly as his or her life proceeds and duties are carried out.

2. *Institutional Knowledge.* The nature of a new professional's work varies greatly among institutions, given their obvious differences (i.e., between the small private college, the community college, and the large public university). Even broader differences may exist in mission, tradition, and culture among outwardly similar institutions. A new professional must understand institution-

al context and account for it in applying professional and legal standards. The same colleague quoted above offers:

When I began working in student affairs, I approached my efforts from a perspective narrowly connected to how I thought things should be done without regard to the history and tenets of the institution where I was working. The ensuing conflict could have been avoided if I had followed the adage: Seek first to understand, then to be understood.

Thus, it is essential for new professionals to gain access to a full range of information. This necessitates a continual effort to understand oneself, one's institution, the accepted guidelines of the profession, and the law. In addition, it is important to note that these knowledge bases are not only interconnected but dynamic as well. As a result, new professionals must be attentive to information sources, their interplay, and their fluctuations in an effort to shape behaviors effectively in and out of the work environment (Elfrink & Coldwell, 1993).

Maintain Integrity. Consistency of character and relationships—integrity—is essential to life and work for all people. Discussions of ethics within the profession often turn to a well-worn phrase: "Do no harm." Although this may be an essential concern, it requires greater clarification than is frequently offered. Several basic ideals, which presumably underlie such an outcome, must be developed in order to enhance the welfare of those served by new professionals.

1. *The individuality* of each person is a foundational principle of operation for new professionals. People live in communities marked by relationships of all sorts. The rights of others and their communities must be respected, yet all must be free to make their own decisions about life issues, their own thoughts, and various ways of expressing them. New professionals must respect the individuality of students and peers and avoid coercing others and unduly limiting their options.

2. *Honesty and truthfulness* are basic to relationships with others. New professionals who are dishonest or unscrupulous undermine their effectiveness with students and peers. If new professionals are not truthful or cannot be counted upon to do what they say they will do, seeds of dissension will be sown and working relationships will be damaged. New professionals are wise to let "yes" be "yes," so far as it lies in their power to do so.

Honesty and truthfulness also demand that new professionals not promise more than they can deliver. This starts in the interview process, where often the tendency is to promise whatever it takes to get the job. This is not truthful, however, and common sense says that it is unwise because it puts a new professional in a very awkward position if held to these promises. Similarly, promotional materials must maintain truthfulness or they will inappropriately promise what cannot be delivered. Truth in advertising is a useful catch phrase because it gives those who enroll or participate in a program an accurate set of expectations and a realistic possibility for fulfilling them.

3. *Confidentiality and trustworthiness*, arguably the complementary counterparts to honesty and truthfulness, are vital ideals for new professionals to pursue. Note the retrospective observation of one new professional from a private institution in the Midwest:

It was sobering to see just how my lack of confidentiality undercut my credibility with peers and institutional leaders. It was a hard way to learn an important lesson.

If one promises to keep something in confidence, that promise must be kept. This is a significant matter for new professionals who must conscientiously work to avoid gossip and violation of confidences in the daily course of their work.

4. *Discretion* is a complex but important virtue for new professionals. To be discrete does not simply mean to be "secretive;" rather, new professionals must be discerning, forthright, and above reproach. The following story from a (male) student affairs administrator who recently was promoted provides a humorous, but notable, anecdote:

Striving to navigate the balance between "hanging out" with students and "maintaining professional distance" can be tricky. I was traveling back to campus after a winter camping experience with two vans full of male students. The eight hour trip was fairly boring so the men thought "mooning" one another (from van to van) would help quicken the time. Inevitably, the group in my van began chanting my name to participate in "the ritual." With mixed feelings, I declined. About six months later, one of the seniors on the trip related how impressed he had been that I had developed a level of relationship with all the men on the trip that would make them feel comfortable asking me to participate in the mooning incident, but yet I had the judgment to know that it would have been inappropriate and would have made everyone uncomfortable had I actually participated. The truth is that I got lucky since I hadn't reasoned the situation out nearly as well as this senior had interpreted it!

Vested interests, financial matters, and sexual relationships are other critical areas where discretion is required. New professionals should distance themselves from conflicts of interest wherever possible and disclose possible conflicts where they unavoidably exist. Not only should the petty cash box be monitored with accurate accounting, but consensual sexual relationships between colleagues or with students should be approached with great care due to the significant potential for misunderstanding. When they do occur, these relationships should be handled with honesty and trustworthiness.

5. *Referrals* are a final practice associated with the principle of maintaining integrity. There is sometimes a tendency among new professionals to seek to expand their abilities and experience by attempting to handle every situation. For example, a new counseling professional at an eastern university stated:

I was flattered when a student so quickly confided in me, telling me about a deep-seated family problem that was significantly affecting her ability to function. My initial response was to marshal all of my graduate training and personal skills on her behalf. Unfortunately, it was only when she became more confused and quit therapy that I realized I should have referred her to another, more experienced colleague.

New professionals must be prepared to refer matters beyond their respective levels of experience or competence to others who can better address specific matters—medical professionals, clinical psychotherapists, clergy, financial advisors, and more experienced peers, among others.

In summary, maintaining integrity demands respect for the individuality of students and peers, honesty, confidentiality, discretion, and the wisdom to make appropriate referrals. As rare as integrity is in our day, new professionals with integrity may serve effectively as "wise friends" (Willimon, 1993, p. 1018) to students and peers alike.

Practice Justice. The daily work of new professionals involves practicing justice. At first glance, this may seem appropriate given the student disciplinarian role that many new professionals perform. On closer inspection, however, it is important to see that justice cannot be an element of this particular task alone but must be part of most, if not all, functions of a new professional. The importance of just practice in the student affairs profession is illustrated below by focusing on three specific functions of justice.

1. *Equity* is a common standard in North American society. Equal treatment of people regardless of race, gender, religion, disability, sexual orientation, or socio-economic status is a foundational principle in all fields. Equity means that people ought to receive even-handed treatment regardless of their uniqueness or distinctiveness, but it is not always that simple. As Kitchener (1985) explains, competing interests must often be balanced, and individual differences must often be taken into account, which can easily lead to justified inequities to compensate for shortcomings and disabilities. These are often difficult decisions to make. Yet the art of practicing justice must be continually a goal.

2. Another important aspect of practicing justice is *impartiality*. New professionals must deal with students and peers in an impartial manner. Neither preference nor prejudice can be shown to various parties without compromising justice and trust. A new resident hall director from a public university makes the following point:

My friendship with the hall leadership made it very difficult to be impartial when several of them violated institutional standards that I was required to enforce. Yet, it was clear that I had to be impartial or I would undercut both my friendship with them and my credibility as the resident director for all of the students.

Impartiality is related to individuality in that people must be respected, not given favor or denied equal treatment. There is a human tendency, however, to form opinions that shape our treatment of others. New professionals must make every effort to avoid showing preference or deference to students or peers in spite of the desire to affirm friends and avoid strangers or those considered "other."

3. *Consistency* is an essential aspect of being just. "Inconsistent justice" is an oxymoron. Justice requires a sense of the wholeness or togetherness of the fabric of actions and decisions. If rules and policies are in place, they ought to be enforced in a consistent manner. Consistency demands that small matters not be ignored one day and big issues the next, or that one person or group be held to a standard different from others. Inconsistency will erode trust, betray impartiality, and violate equity; it is antithetical to the kind of management and relationships that affirm people and establish justice.

Interpersonal conflicts in the workplace offer one of the common arenas in which practicing justice is important. New professionals frequently find themselves in the midst of interpersonal conflicts with students or colleagues and must navigate these waters carefully. Regularly standing for equity, impartiality, and consistency assists new professionals in addressing such conflicts. When they do occur, great care must be taken to ensure that one does not use position to enforce a biased solution. When intervening in interpersonal conflicts, new professionals also do well to remain impartial and to seek justice, not simply accommodation. Otherwise, the problem often recurs in another form at a later time. Sorting through the baggage that various parties bring to such conflicts may be tedious, but it is crucial.

Although practicing justice for some new professionals most frequently takes the form of adjudication (e.g., resolving a violation of a student conduct code), it includes much more. For example, within the larger institutional context, practicing justice is an important consideration in the hiring process. First, the posting of a vacancy itself must be just. Are posted jobs truly available as advertised? Are the qualifications and the range of responsibilities accurately listed? Is the vacancy really open to all applicants, or are specific preferences clearly stated along with a supporting rationale? Second, the process of consideration must be just. Will candidates be given the opportunity to demonstrate their qualifications for the position? Will they be given equal consideration, regardless of race, gender, religion, disability, sexual orientation, or socio-economic status? Will communication with all candidates be equitable, efficient, and impartial? Finally, the salary and benefits offered must be equitable within the institution (and the profession). Differentiation based on education or experience is normal, but other forms of discrimination are unjust. New professionals must make every effort to practice justice in hiring and in personnel matters.

Practicing justice is also a relevant issue in new professionals' direct work with students. That is, being just necessitates that new professionals affirm students' individuality as well as their common traits. On the one hand, affirming the individuality of students requires recognizing the uniqueness of students' backgrounds and needs and responding to them through programming, services, advocacy, and interventions. To do otherwise is to treat all students as the same and, from our perspective, sacrifices justice in the process. On the other hand, new professionals must acknowledge that all students have common needs (e.g., safety) and common personal attributes (e.g., cognition) and then actively seek to meet these common needs effectively. Ultimately, if new professionals fail to recognize that students have common needs, attempt to meet these common needs inappropriately or poorly, ignore students' common personal attributes, or take no initiative to assist students in these common areas of human development, justice is compromised.

A final word about practicing justice in the student affairs profession. Justice is a lofty goal, but it is important that the means as well as the ends be just. It is tempting to look at a situation and determine a desired result; navigating a just course to arrive at that outcome is another matter. Great care must be taken to ensure that new professionals do not sacrifice procedural justice in an effort to achieve a just conclusion. To do so is to undermine the commitment to justice that must underlie the whole process and to violate the integrity of the process.

In summary, being informed, maintaining integrity, and practicing justice involve personal, institutional, professional, and legal dynamics that must be explored and applied in the warp and woof of daily student affairs efforts. There also must be congruity in how student affairs professionals work out these principles in various contexts. A new professional working in student activities underscores the difficulty of establishing such congruity:

The challenge for me is that my system of beliefs may not always mesh with the beliefs of colleagues, supervisors, and the institution in which I work. For example, what I view as just is not necessarily what my institution views as just. The dilemma then is how to maintain justice to self and justice to the institution.

Notwithstanding what this new professional refers to as "the challenge," new professionals must seek to harmonize how they practice justice personally, institutionally, professionally, and legally. Conversely, the contours of being informed, maintaining integrity, and practicing justice will be defined according to the particular institutional context in which these principles are practiced.

43

HYPOTHETICAL SCENARIOS

Now that we have outlined a framework and some guiding principles for the ethic and ethics of new professionals, it may be useful to examine how they may be put into operation. Fictional scenarios, representing possible real-life situations that a new professional may confront, are presented below. The paragraphs that follow each scenario spin out several ways that it may relate to a new professional's ethic as well as some of the principles that may come into play. Read the briefs and consider how the matter could be addressed. Then look at the perspectives and questions raised in the subsequent explanatory paragraphs.

Brief #1

Four finalists have been interviewed for a job and the selection committee, on which you serve, has found two candidates well qualified for the job. The committee reached consensus on who is the better candidate of the two, but you have personal knowledge that this candidate is gay. Although this is a public institution that does not discriminate based on sexual orientation, your concern is that two of your colleagues will have significant difficulty working for a gay supervisor. Since hiring this person will cause conflict in your division, how should you proceed? Should you press for the second best candidate to avoid conflict among your colleagues? Should you talk privately with the dean of your division, alerting her to the possible problems involved with hiring the candidate whom you know to be gay? Can you opt to do nothing?

It is clear that the gay candidate is perceived by the search committee to be the best person for the job. The process identified him as such and both integrity and justice require that he be offered the position. Professional guidelines and the law concur, both of which are reinforced by the public mission of the institution. There are also other matters entering into the discussion. First, there is the matter of confidentiality and discretion. Do you have the obligation to keep secret what the candidate did not reveal in the interview process? Is the candidate's sexual orientation a matter of public record if you have personal knowledge of it? Will you be acting in a trustworthy manner if you reveal the candidate's sexual orientation—or if you do not reveal it? Which is an honest way to proceed? Second, there is the issue of equity. If people are passed over due to sexual orientation, is the process equitable? A related third issue is impartiality. Will not preferences and prejudices be operating if the top candidate is denied the job? The fourth issue is the consideration of truth in advertising. Did the position posting state that it was not open to gay men? If not, how can a person be eliminated for reasons related to sexual orientation? A final issue is consistency. Needless to say, articulating a non-discrimination policy while at the same time discriminating is clearly inconsistent.

Given a different new professional serving on the search committee, or a different institution, profession, or legal code, this case may be construed quite differently. Consider a different institutional context. A private institution may develop its hiring policy in accordance with its mission to obligate applicants to uphold and abide by certain moral or religious principles. In such a case, sexual orientation requirements may be clearly articulated and used as a basis of judgment in decision-making. Accordingly, the new professional may be acting in a completely ethical manner in choosing between candidates on such a basis. In such an institution, a new professional perhaps should feel compelled to make such a decision—regardless of the sentiments of the majority of the committee. In every case, a new professional's ethic and ethics are a complex mix of personal, institutional, professional, and legal contexts.

Brief #2

Your small college is experiencing significant financial difficulty, due in large measure to an overtaxed financial aid program. The dean of enrollment management redesigned the admissions policy to ensure that those with more financial resources are admitted and enrolled instead of those less able to pay, as many higher education institutions are doing in this new fiscal environment. Instead of using merit criteria alone for admissions and wait-list decisions, ability to pay will now be a significant factor in admissions decisions in an attempt to relieve the college's fiscal difficulties. As a new professional, finishing your first year as an admissions counselor at this institution, you are faced with a dilemma. Your graduate training has convinced you that such a practice is unfair to less financially endowed students who are well qualified for admission. Moreover, you know that such practice violates the Standards of Good Practice for the National Association of College Admissions Counselors (NACAC) to which the college ascribes. What recourse do you have as a new professional? What obligations, if any, do you have? Should you discuss this matter with the dean of enrollment management, forget it, or look for a new job?

This situation is one faced by many colleges and universities in our day, as financial exigencies come to the fore, and it must be addressed squarely and honestly. First, there is the matter of professional and legal standards. Is it legal and appropriate to base admissions decisions on ability to pay? It appears to be legal, but professional guidelines, like NACAC Principles of Good Practice, caution against using financial ability as a test for admission. At the same time, there is much debate in the profession as to whether this is a good principle when institutions are no longer able or willing to meet fully the financial needs of the students whom they admit. The profession is in the midst of change. Some argue, on the basis of professional principles or personal morality, that it is unfair to admit a student without also supplying the means to finance enrollment. Although the available options are all legal, personal and institutional contexts seem to press for changes in long-standing professional practice, and this case illustrates the dynamic nature of personal and institutional contexts. Now more than ever, new professionals must consider and apply ethical principles to chart the course ahead, underscoring the need to pay attention to the particular contexts in which the issue must be considered.

At this point, principles like truthfulness, equity, impartiality, and consistency again come into play within a particular institutional context. Concern for the institution seems paramount in the case presented; that is, addressing the financial aid budget. There is a real tension between the ideals of equity and impartiality and the financial stability of the institution. If the policy change goes forward, how will admissions decisions be made that are equitable and impartial? Similarly, how will financial ability be weighed in the balance of academic ability and other factors of suitability for admission? Further, will prospective students be told that these decisions are being made in an effort to have "truth in advertising?" More simply, what will prospective students be told at all? How will new professionals feel about their role in shaping the composition of the student body under this kind of admission policy? How will academic integrity be maintained? Will an adequate number of qualified students with financial ability apply? Will others refuse to bother because they remain unconvinced that their perception of inequity is mistaken? This is a complex issue that reaches into the core of the ethic of the student affairs profession. When one considers that personal commitments and professional legacies are also intimately connected to this issue, it is easy to see how complex these issues really are. At some point, a new professional may even decide to seek employment more compatible with his or her personal or professional ethic.

CONCLUSION

It is impossible to cover all facets of ethic and ethics development in a single chapter. The emerging issues facing new professionals today require them to take seriously the responsibility to develop an ethic and ethics that equip them to address issues in an informed manner, while maintaining integrity and practicing justice in personal, institutional, professional, and legal contexts. New professionals who consciously develop their ethic before the hard cases present themselves will be ready for the rough-and-tumble of everyday ethical decision-making. Probing the contexts, principles, and ideals of ethical decision-making is a helpful way to work out one's ethic and we encourage it. Understanding the personal, institutional, professional, and legal dimensions of ethic development is essential as well.

The new professional, however, need not be limited to themes in this chapter in developing ethical insight and experience. Talk to peers about ethical dilemmas and how they can be navigated. Work out better responses for future instances of those same dilemmas. Subscribe to periodicals such as *Synthesis:*

Law and Policy in Higher Education or *The College Student and the Courts,* or examine one of the recent books on the subject (e.g., Fried, 1997; Young, 1997) to explore ethical and legal issues in higher education. Take time to initiate frank discussions with supervisors and others in your institution about ethical matters that they anticipate you will face and their suggestions for ways to address them—and do not be satisfied with canned answers or unlikely resolutions to real problems. In addition, it may be instructive for new professionals to consult the work of ethicists themselves as they elaborate ethical decision-making processes. In this regard, Kidder's (1995) "Ethical Checkpoints" may be helpful as well as Nash's (1989) "12 Questions." We have included Nash's "12 Questions" below to provide a glimpse of how ethicists may approach ethical decision-making in the workplace:

• Have you defined the problem accurately?
• How would you define the problem if you stood on the other side of the fence?
• How did the situation occur in the first place?
• To whom and to what do you give your loyalties as a person or group and as a member of the organization?
• What is your intention in making this decision?
• How does this intention (#5) compare with the likely results?
• Whom could your decision or action injure?
• Can you engage the affected parties in a discussion of the problem before you make your decision?
• Are you confident that your position will be as valid for a long period as it seems now?
• Could you disclose without qualm your decision or action to your boss, your CEO, the board of directors, your family, or society as a whole?
• What is the symbolic potential of your action if understood? Misunderstood?
• Under what conditions would you allow exceptions to your stand?

Whether you anticipate them or not, be assured that ethical dilemmas will confront you in this profession. An ethical character sensitized and habituated to "doing the right thing" will assist you in more successfully working with students, peers, and supervisors in a manner that is well informed and manifests integrity and justice. Only then will new professionals be well equipped to strive for what is best for all, which is far better than simply "doing no harm."

REFERENCES

American College Personnel Association (1989). *A statement of ethical principles and standards*. Alexandria, VA: Author.

Bellah, R., Madsen, R., Sullivan, W., Swidler, A., & Tipton, S. (1992). *The good society*. NY: Vintage.

Canon, H. J. (1989). Guiding standards and principles. In U. Delworth, G. Hanson, & Associates (Eds.), *Student services: A handbook for the profession* (2nd ed., pp. 57-79). San Francisco: Jossey-Bass.

Canon, H. J. (1993). Maintaining high ethical standards. In M. J. Barr & Associates (Eds.), *The handbook of student affairs administration* (pp. 327-339). San Francisco: Jossey-Bass.

Coleman, D. D., & Johnson, J. E. (Eds.). (1990). *The new professional* (NASPA Monograph Series, Vol. 10). Washington, DC: National Association of Student Personnel Administrators.

Council for the Advancement of Standards for Student Services/Development Programs. . (1986). *CAS standards and guidelines for student services/development programs*. Washington, DC: Author.

Dalton, J. C. (1993). Organizational imperatives for implementing the essential values. In R. Young (Ed.), *Identifying and implementing the essential values of the profession*. New Directions for Student Services, No. 61 (pp. 87-96). San Francisco: Jossey-Bass.

Elfrink, V., & Coldwell, L. (1993). Values in decision making: The INVOLVE model. In R. Young (Ed.), *Identifying and implementing the essential values of the profession*. New Directions for Student Services, No. 61 (pp. 62-73). San Francisco: Jossey-Bass.

Fried, J. (Ed.). (1997). *Contemporary ethical issues for student affairs*. New Directions for Student Services, No. 77. San Francisco: Jossey-Bass.

Kerr, C. (1994). Comment on the special problem of teaching about ethics. In C. Kerr, *Troubled times for American higher education* (pp. 147-156). Albany, NY: SUNY Press.

Kidder, R. M. (1995). *How good people make tough choices: Resolving the dilemmas of ethical living*. New York: Fireside.

Kitchener, K. S. (1985). Ethical principles and ethical decisions in student affairs. In H. Canon & R. Brown (Eds.), *Applied ethics in student services*. New Directions for Student Services, No. 30 (pp. 17-30). San Francisco: Jossey-Bass.

Nash, L. L. (1989). Ethics without the sermon. In K. R. Andrews (Ed.), *Ethics in practice: Managing the moral corporation* (pp. 243-257). Boston: Harvard Business School Press.

National Association of Student Personnel Administrators. (1990). *Statement of principles and ethical practices of student personnel administrators.* Portland, OR: Author.

Rickard, S. T. (1993). Truth, freedom, justice: Academic tradition and the essential values. In R. Young (Ed.), *Identifying and implementing the essential values of the profession.* New Directions for Student Services, No. 61 (pp. 15-23). San Francisco: Jossey-Bass.

Willimon, W. (1993, Oct. 20). Reaching and teaching the abandoned generation. *Christian Century,* 110, pp. 1016-1019.

Winston, Jr., R. B., & McCaffrey, S. S. (1983). Ethical practice in student affairs administration. In T. Miller, R. Winston, Jr., & W. Mendenhall (Eds.), *Administration and leadership in student affairs* (pp. 167-191). Muncie, IN: Accelerated Development.

Winston, R. B., Jr., & Saunders, S. A. (1991). Ethical professional practice in student affairs. In T. Miller, R. Winston, Jr. & Associates (Eds.), *Administration and leadership in student affairs* (2nd ed., pp. 309-345). Muncie, IN: Accelerated Development.

Winston, R. B., Jr., Anchors, S., & Associates. (1993). *Student housing and residential life.* San Francisco: Jossey-Bass.

Young, R. B. (Ed.). (1993). The essential values of the profession. In R. Young (Ed.), *Identifying and implementing the essential values of the profession.* New Directions in Student Services, No. 61 (pp. 5-13). San Francisco: Jossey-Bass.

Young, R. B. (1997). *No neutral ground: Standing by the values we prize in higher education.* San Francisco: Jossey-Bass.

CHAPTER 4

Supervisory Style: The Photographer Within

RANDI S. SCHNEIDER

New student affairs professionals come to their positions with varying levels of training in supervision. Some are not actually new professionals, having had supervisory experience outside student affairs, while others begin supervising without previous professional experience. In either case, the complexity of supervising student affairs staff requires an ability both to adopt a flexible approach to supervision using multiple perspectives and to communicate effectively across the many disciplines from which people come to this profession (Dalton, 1996).

Unfortunately, student affairs graduate coursework and practical experience typically do little to enhance these abilities or to provide the background necessary to support early success in a supervisory role (Schuh & Carlisle, 1991). While some graduate programs provide opportunities for on-the-job supervisory training through assistantships, trial by fire is often the primary training tool. As one new resident director wrote: "When I started working, I was thrown into supervision without any real training. It is as if the department said, 'Here is your staff—do what you want.'" This chapter attempts to fill this gap in professional preparation by focusing on using multiple perspectives in the supervision of student affairs staff.

Not surprisingly, there is no single body of knowledge that encompasses supervision. Since academic preparation, practical experience, values, cultural background, and style preferences differ from person to person, supervision is a complex process requiring approaches tailored to each situation, individual, or team. As such, an understanding and an appreciation of multiple perspectives can be useful to the supervisor in student affairs.

Schuh and Carlisle (1991) define supervision as the "relationship where one person has the responsibility to provide leadership, direction, information, motivation, evaluation, or support for one or more persons" (p. 497). For the purpose of this chapter, Bolman and Deal's (1991) organizational leadership issues are added to this definition in order to encourage multiple perspectives on supervision. Bolman and Deal challenge leaders to broaden their organizational perspective by developing a wider range of choices in their leadership repertoire. Supervisors must consider their role in light of organizational structure, human resources, politics, and the culture of the organization. Therefore, supervision, as used in this chapter, is: *The formal relationship of one person to another where there is a prescribed role requiring one person to provide to another leadership, direction, appropriate resources, evaluation, and support within the context of an historically based institutional culture and structured hierarchy.* Though closely related, the prescriptive formality of the supervisory relationship is what differentiates leadership from supervision.

Much of this chapter relies on Bolman and Deal's (1991) four-framed organizational model. Like the lens of a camera, each frame offers a new set of ideas, values, and emphases from which to view the many issues a supervisor faces. The structural frame looks at formal roles and responsibilities, including rules, policies, and management hierarchies. The human resources frame focuses on the needs of individuals within the organization. The political frame is an analysis of how people and groups interact and compete (or both) in the organization for scarce resources. The symbolic frame analyzes the symbols, myths, and rituals that provide the roots for much of what happens within an organization. The four frames can be discussed as separate organizational issues, but, in reality, it is the combination of the four perspectives that constitutes the dynamics of the workplace.

SUPERVISORS AS ARCHITECTS

The leader who sees the organization primarily through a structural frame is considered an architect. This type of leader focuses on the design and analysis of the organizational infrastructure (Bolman & Deal, 1991). In organizations, responsibilities are allocated to participants (division of labor), and rules, policies, and management hierarchies are created to coordinate diverse activities. Structures are the organizational elements that are seen (such as operations manual), the things that are measured (such as quantitative data), and the things that can be defined (such as a policy or the chain of command). All effective supervisors, in some way, must serve as architects. Whether your role is to supervise peer educators, resident assistants, orientation leaders, support staff, graduate assistants, or student affairs professionals, the supervisor's obligation is to provide and use the structures that support success. This is apparent in the words of one new professional from a counseling resource center:

I started my job and had two weeks before being thrown to the wolves. The coordinator of training believed the most important part of training was team building. Unfortunately, that did not help me get ready for the task of providing educational programming to a campus with 15,000 students. I wanted to know the policies, procedures, and information necessary for doing my job. By the time my students arrived on campus, I was so stressed I could not think clearly.

To reduce ambiguity, organizational structures often provide a fixed division of labor (Kuh, 1996). The distribution of a position description and an organizational chart assists staff members in understanding their role in the organization and seeing how those roles fit within a department. A supervisor must also articulate basic expectations for the successful accomplishment of a particular job (Career Press, 1993). Performance guidelines help reduce the ambiguity that staff members feel in a new job or when starting to work for a new supervisor. Among the issues that relate to the structural aspect of supervision are the importance of documenting activity, following policies and procedures, working with unionized employees, and hiring staff.

Documentation. An essential element of structure is the documenting of organizational and supervisory activity. Documentation plays many roles in an organization, from maintaining records of important conversations to providing needed information for program planning. While a supervisor's emerging style and the organization's history will dictate when the documentation of personnel concerns is appropriate, a new professional should avoid underestimating the role that documentation plays in performance review. Maintaining adequate documentation and completing required forms can help avoid misunderstandings in personnel decisions. In extreme cases, when staff performance leads a supervisor to consider disciplinary action, proper documentation saves time and frustration. Without documentation, supervisors must recreate history and may be unable to take disciplinary action due to lack of a proper paper trail. Documentation also provides an excellent written record of support for salary increases and promotions. Sending a letter to document a behavioral problem or simply to say thanks is all part of supervision.

Supervisors must also understand the appropriate role of documentation in the culture of the organization and adjust their style to meet its needs:

The first time I sent a follow-up memo to my boss documenting a meeting and our discussion, he came into my office, threw it on my desk, and accused me of not trusting him. From that point on, I kept follow-up memos in my personal files much like a diary. [Assistant Dean]

If the department's tradition is such that the need for documentation does not exist, a supervisor emphasizing documentation may be seen as untrusting or overzealous. Likewise, a supervisor who has a low need for documentation may be seen as lazy and irresponsible in an organization where documentation is expected. If an organizational motto is, "if it is not in writing, it did not happen," supervisors who rely upon informal verbal communication may experience frustration. This example also points out how the frames through which the supervisory role is viewed—in this case structural and cultural—interact with and influence each other.

Perhaps one of the most interesting documentation issues to emerge in the last decade is the management of electronic communication. Electronic mail can be a documentation and communication tool, or it can be a nuisance. Organizations that rely heavily on documentation may overuse electronic communication.

As a Complex Director I receive approximately 70 e-mails per day. The central office staff, my RDs, and my colleagues send me anything anyone believes may have some value. My supervisor feels strongly that we should read and respond to e-mail at least three times per day. I spend many hours at my computer and following up on e-mail related issues. It is an efficient way to communicate, but hardly an effective use of my time. I estimate that 50% of the e-mail I receive is the professional equivalent of spam. In the days of telephones and paper, I would have lived without the information with no consequence.

Labor Unions. Among the most structured of supervisory relationships are those that involve working with members of labor unions. Even for supervisors trained in the area of labor relations, the potential for conflict is significant. Some new supervisors resist the structures that are firmly in place for labor union affiliated employees, but it is incumbent upon them to become educated about the collective bargaining agreements involving their staff. Supervisors of unionized employees must understand that the policies and procedures negotiated into the labor contract are designed to protect those covered by the agreements. Two of the most basic values underlying labor agreements are due process and individual rights (Carnevale & Stone, 1995); both are also values underpinning higher education (Carnegie Foundation, 1990). Contracts are often strictly enforced; ignorance of the rules is not an appropriate excuse for noncompliance. There is little room for ambiguity in the interpretation of a labor contract. This scenario is common:

I supervise 10 staff members who are from a collective bargaining unit. I have many years of experience in my profession but this is the first time I have supervised unionized staff. In the beginning I found it very difficult to hold staff accountable to my expectations and blamed the labor agreement specifications. However, I quickly learned the importance of the content of the labor agreement. I needed to learn that if accountability was a goal for me that I would need to be unfailing in my approach to establishing and documenting expectations, being consistent in my management of issues, never take anything personally, and document, document, document. [Health Center]

Recommendations for avoiding grievance problems include understanding union contracts, promoting good relationships with the union steward and staff, maintaining a fair work environment, keeping an open mind when conflicts arise, and using appropriate investigation skills when resolving conflicts (Career Press, 1993). In extreme cases, when a unionized employee is not performing up to expected standards, it can feel difficult to work within the labor contract to hold the employee accountable. A supervisor with just cause to confront a unionized staff member must also be ready to deal with the bureaucracy and the conflict. It is easy to fall into an "us versus them" mentality when dealing with unionized staff, particularly in times of conflict, but that merely erects another barrier. It is important to realize that unions exist to protect their employees, and that professionals must work with them accordingly.

Hiring Practice and Policy. Hiring new staff is the most important way to shape the future of an organization. Part of supervision is participating in search and selection procedures; part of hiring is knowing the expectations and practices outlined by law, organizational policy, and our profession's ethical standards. This section does not address this issue in depth other than to indicate that a new professional must be aware of the laws and policies related to hiring. For instance, supervisors must consider institution- and unit-specific hiring policies. If a department has a personnel officer, that person often will have a working knowledge of how the hiring procedures fit into the framework of legal practice. This person is important to know, especially for a new professional involved in hiring for the first time in a particular organization. If there is no human resources officer or supervisor with knowledge of proper practice, and a new supervisor has questions about the hiring process (time lines, forms, documentation, letters, etc.), the campus human resources or affirmative action office can likely assist in reviewing hiring plans. New professionals who supervise student staff members should keep in mind that, on some campuses, the hiring and firing of student staff is considered minor in comparison to issues related to professional staff and faculty, but it is expected that practice will be within the ethical standards of field. (See Chapter 3 for further discussion of ethics.)

SUPERVISOR AS CATALYST

Bolman and Deal's (1991) second organizational frame is human resources. Supervisors who are good managers of human resources are seen as catalysts, because they promote high performance among staff members. The human resource frame, based on the concepts and research of organizational and social psychology, starts with the premise that organizations are made up of individuals who have needs, feelings, prejudices, skills, and limitations. From a human resource perspective, the key to effectiveness is to tailor organizations to people while addressing these underlying issues (Bolman & Deal, 1991). The effective supervisor empowers and supports personnel so they may reach the highest levels of personal and professional achievement. An effective catalyst knows how to lead and serve the people within the framework of expectations, procedures, and policies established by effective organizational architects.

While the architect's metaphor for an effective organization is that of the well-oiled machine, the catalyst sees the organization as organic—as alive and growing. In student affairs, building effective teams is really a process of bringing out the best in the people who work in the organization. Effective supervisors know that the individual personalities of their staff members are as important as their job descriptions. The catalyst recognizes that when there is a good fit between the person and the organization, both benefit. The following example from a new professional combines the issues related to good fit with those related to the structure of the organization:

When I started working in student activities at [institution], I was overwhelmed. I had gone to a school where nobody cared about rules. There are so many policies, so many procedures, and so many rules where I work now. My boss is kind and gives me as much help as he can. But I am not happy and need to leave so I can work in an environment that emphasizes the person over the paper. [Student Activities Programmer]

From the perspective of an architect, it is important to understand policy and from the perspective of a catalyst, to understand the people the policy affects. The dynamics of human interaction can provide excellent supervisory learning experiences and growth for both the leader and the followers. Among the skills and issues associated with the human resources frame are communication, training and development, cross-cultural supervision, and performance review.

Communication. Effective communication skills are among the greatest assets of a supervisor (or any employee). Paying attention to and effectively communicating with staff members is a foundational skill in supervision. Staff members have important things to say, may know more about what is happening in the organization (or with students) than their supervisor, and may feel much better about their role in the organization if they know their supervisor is listening. Communication, when carried out effectively, is a two-way street.

Research shows that when employees are given an opportunity to participate actively in their work environment and to have their ideas heard, significant improvements occur in both morale and productivity (Bolman & Deal, 1991), as noted in the experience of this new professional:

I never felt like my perspective while working at [institution] was valued. My colleagues and I spent hours talking about the lack of input we had into our department. In my new job, I feel like my input is valued. I can give you 100 reasons why I prefer coming to work now that I feel valued as a person. Now when I go out with my colleagues we rarely talk about work in a negative way. We talk about our families, our vacation plans, or funny things that happened to us at the office. [Financial Aid Counselor]

Delegation as Staff Development. Most professionals like their jobs to provide autonomy, variety, challenge, and enjoyment. Supervisors must learn how to delegate interesting projects to staff members who are ready for new challenges. Often, the only way to find out if people are ready for new challenges is to ask or to provide the challenge and monitor the results. Delegating a project is particularly difficult for supervisors who like to maintain a high level of control. The ability to provide appropriate guidance on a project (based on the skill level of the staff) without being too controlling is a difficult balance to achieve but an important skill to learn. Even so, supervisors should remember that the more people they have doing innovative and interesting work, the more productive their staff and department become. It reflects positively on the supervisor and provides excellent experience to the staff. If the supervisor is the only person doing innovative projects, the whole team suffers.

> **Avoiding grievance problems include[s] understanding labor law and contracts, promoting good relationships with union stewards, maintaining a fair work environment, keeping an open mind… and using appropriate investigation skills when resolving conflicts.**

Staff Training and Development. Kaufman (1994) views the human resources of an organization as *human capital.* This idea parallels traditional notions of organizational capital, which refer to the financial resources available to corporations and other organizations. Kaufman (1994) argues that investing in human capital is important in order to have a high quality labor force and an effective organization. When supervisors invest in their employees—including helping them to gain greater skills, increase their knowledge, and maintain good health—the investment results in a happier, more highly skilled, more motivated, and more effective work force. The investment involves reallocating work time for education and training (Kaufman, 1994). For new supervisors this means that staff training programs should include helping people improve their job performance (e.g., how to program, how to advise a student group, how to handle a disciplinary referral) and grow in areas outside their jobs (e.g., personal wellness, career advancement). Good training and development programs take into consideration the needs of the organization and the needs of the individuals. Training and development can occur in group settings (e.g., formal time for staff development in the weekly schedule) or individually. Allow time during one-on-one supervision meetings to discuss ways that you, as a supervisor, can enhance the professional development of each staff member by creating individualized learning opportunities.

Supervision and Multicultural Issues. Cross-cultural supervision can be challenging. Performance issues must be treated in a fair and consistent manner, without regard to factors such as gender, race, sexual orientation, or disability. If a supervisor is uncomfortable in a supervisory situation due to some cultural (e.g., racial, ethnic, international) or related (e.g., gender, disability, sexual orientation) difference, it is the supervisor's responsibility to identify the root of his or her discomfort and take appropriate steps to address it. Being selected to supervise others does not eliminate a person's own experience, biases, or stereotypes. In fact, to assume that one does not have biases is perhaps the greatest obstacle to self-learning and effective cross-cultural supervision.

In recognizing the need to learn more about a particular difference (e.g., supervising a deaf staff member for the first time), the supervisor should not place responsibility solely on the staff member but must take the initiative to learn about those who are different. New professionals in supervisory positions, both members of groups in the majority and those who are marginalized in the institution, should reflect on their experiences and assumptions in relation to the supervision of people viewed as culturally or otherwise different from them.

Other issues become evident when trying to transform a department or organization into one that is more culturally inclusive. One new professional's situation illustrates the complexity of trying to address multiple needs of the organization—in this case, staff diversification and consistent policy enforcement:

I worked on a campus that had low African American enrollment and a very hard time recruiting African American RAs. The residential life program wanted to increase its number of African American RAs. The tradition of residence life dictated that all RA staff meetings took place on the same night, and this expectation was made clear during the hiring process. As it turned out, the campus Black Choir held its mandatory practice on the same night and many African American student leaders were members of the Black Choir. On our campus the Black Choir was a primary support mechanism for students. I was approached by several students regarding the possibility of waiving the requirement for attendance at the weekly staff meeting, so that African American students could be involved in the choir, and serve as RAs. [Complex Director]

Bolman and Deal's (1991) framework suggests that the decision whether to waive the attendance requirement or change the meeting time and day can be viewed from several perspectives: structural (e.g., pre-existing policies communicated to all staff, policies to consider future requests for accommodation), human resource (e.g., the needs of the individuals versus the needs of the organization), and cultural (e.g., exploring why the meeting has been traditionally held at on that day and at that time). Although the appropriate course of action is not always clear, focusing on a single perspective provides a limited view that may be subject to biases or assumptions that serve to maintain the status quo.

Performance Review. Investing in human capital means more than providing training and development opportunities for staff members; a supervisor must also find ways to assess their continuing performance. The ability to review performance fairly is an important skill to develop. Student affairs professionals who plan a career path that includes supervision must learn the key supervisory skill of giving both positive and constructive feedback to their staff.

Performance review does not mean the same thing to everyone. A student affairs professional who once worked in a corporate setting had been evaluated on purely measurable criteria. "If I made my goals, I was a good employee." In student affairs, a performance review is often less quantifiable. Additionally, different supervisors use evaluation as a tool to achieve different ends. According to Bolman and Deal (1991), an architect might see the review process as a way of distributing rewards and controlling performance, while a catalyst would see it as a way of helping staff members grow and develop. A supervisor can use the performance review to exercise power in appropriate (to influence) or inappropriate (to manipulate) ways. A review can be an important yearly ritual or a habit that supervisors (and staff) learn to dread. The purpose of performance review and the criteria used to evaluate performance must be communicated to staff members by the supervisor.

Evaluating performance is something that should be part of an on-going feedback loop. The loop does not begin at the performance review. The loop begins on the day staff tasks are defined and expectations are negotiated, continues at every supervisory meeting, leads to the formal performance review, and culminates with the articulation of new staff expectations. Staff members ought to be given an opportunity to provide feedback on the expectations of the organization as well as to appraise their own performance through a self-evaluation.

The annual performance appraisal may be a time to review previous feedback discussions, but it should not be a time to say, "Surprise—I think you are going to get fired." If evaluation material presented to a staff member comes as a surprise, it means that the supervisor is not giving enough on-going feedback. And, while supervisors are busy providing constructive ways for staff members to improve performance, they should also be providing appropriate positive feedback. If giving constructive criticism is difficult, supervisors should consider finding at least one positive for each constructive issue presented. If there is nothing positive to say in a performance review, supervisors should ask themselves: "Why is this person still working for me?" The answer could be political (e.g., a person cannot be fired because he or she is related to a senior administrator) but could as easily be that the supervisor is not providing sufficient structure and feedback.

Additionally, new professionals should determine if their departments provide opportunities for staff members to evaluate them as supervisors. Giving staff members a process by which they can provide feedback to the supervisor is invaluable. If there is no formal mechanism for this type of feedback, one should be created. Few people know the skills, foibles, and vulnerabilities supervisors quite like their own staff. This type of evaluation of the supervisor also provides a positive example of on-going evaluation and self-development.

What staff members believe about evaluation is of equal importance. Even the simple rating scale used in a performance review process can cause stress. On a scale of one to five, it is important to define what a "three" represents. Supervisors should provide staff members with the knowledge they need to understand the "grading" scale. Additionally, it is imperative that supervisors use the grading scale in a consistent manner with members of the staff. The catalyst remembers that performance evaluation has to meet both human resource and organizational needs in order to be effective.

SUPERVISOR AS ADVOCATE

When supervisors invest in their employees—including helping them gain greater skills, increase their knowledge and maintain good health—the investment results in a more effective work force.

A new supervisor who views organizational activity through the political frame realizes that all action is not dictated by policy and all decisions are not made in formal meetings, as would be assumed by someone viewing the world strictly through the structural frame. Viewing the organization through the political frame encourages a focus on how different individuals and interest groups compete for power and for scarce resources in order to influence action and focus energy in an organization. The advocate, or the political supervisor, builds coalitions, serves as spokesperson for his or her staff, and works the formal and informal systems for the benefit of the staff and the whole institution (Bolman & Deal, 1991). All members of an organization interact as political beings. Being apolitical or choosing to remain outside of the political arena is practically impossible and professionally irresponsible given the multiple obligations of the supervisor. The political frame encourages recognition of informal ways of influencing action in the organization in contrast to the structural frame, which focuses on formal means to ends and goals (e.g., through written policies).

In the political frame, supervisors work within systems composed of different interest groups that are constantly involved in bargaining, negotiating, compromising, and occasionally, coercing. For instance, reflect back on the example of the African American students who would like to stay active in the Black Choir and also be RAs. Numerous individuals and groups were involved in that case, each responding from their own needs and from their own perspectives. There are many possibilities for the dynamic interplay of organizational politics when dealing with virtually all decisions of consequence. Professionals in the supervisory role for the first time may be uncomfortable when a major conflict of this sort occurs. Wanting to be liked and to feel good about one's environment and relationships may exacerbate the discomfort, and when conflict arises, there may be an immediate sense of "what have I done wrong?" In the political frame, however, conflict is seen as inevitable, a natural and necessary element in the growth of the organization. When conflict is faced openly and honestly, relationships can build upon trust, and individual and organizational performance can be enhanced.

The Advocate and Power. Some professionals learn to dislike the word *power*, but power can be good or bad, used or abused. Power is the ability to perform or act effectively, to exercise influence or control. Supervisors need to be aware of the various types of power they have or have access to (and the power that others have) in order to enhance their ability to influence organizational action and obtain necessary resources.

The most obvious power available to an organizational member is the power of position, i.e., the formal authority associated with a position in an organizational hierarchy. Even individuals high in the organizational hierarchy, such as directors, deans, and vice presidents, recognize that this type of power is limited and that other forms of power are necessary to influence the staff members they supervise. These include the powers associated with information, rewards, and access.

The power of information. Information is the lifeblood of an organization and of the individuals within that organization: information about resources, budgets, expectations, perceptions, outcomes, goals, changes, organizational history, and priorities. Having, controlling, and filtering information is an inevitable aspect of organizational life. Supervisors are conduits for information flowing through an organization. And, while information flow may be seen as a structural matter—information flows up and down the hierarchy—all information is filtered in the process of communication. When information is selectively disseminated to influence decisions, it becomes a political tool. New professional supervisors must be aware of the importance of information and seek it out in order to enhance their performance and the performance of their staff. When supervisors recognize that all information is, inevitably, filtered and incomplete, they become more proactive in clarifying the data they receive and seeking the data they do not have. Supervisors are better able to do their jobs when they obtain and pass on necessary information to their staff members.

Consider the plight of the complex director concerned about the volume of electronic mail received. Some of that mail, in the eyes of the CD, is a documentation nightmare. In the eyes of the central office staff, that same e-mail may be seen as the fastest way to empower staff with knowledge. Here are some thoughts to consider when making choices about electronic communication:

- E-mail is not confidential or private. What if your e-mail were posted to the entire university, stolen by a hacker or used in a court of law?
- Be concise. Are you making your point and being mindful of the receiver's time?
- Use subject lines that assist the reader in prioritizing and organizing. What does "stuff about work" mean?
- Do not overuse reply to all or send mass mailings when a targeted e-mail would suffice. Who needs to know?
- Respond to e-mail in a timely fashion (2-3 days). Do you like waiting?
- Request delivery receipts only if documentation is essential. Use the high priority option in your electronic mail program sparingly. Will you be seen as the organization's Chicken Little if everything is urgent?
- Civility is as important in electronic communication as it is in face-to-face communication. If you are angry, frustrated, or hurt, is it a good idea to push "send"?
- Depending upon the circumstances, e-mail can be a reflection of professional writing skills. Can you differentiate between the circumstances that call for a well-developed document versus e-chatting?
- Be mindful of the chain of command in the organization when sending e-mail. Who is on your "cc list" and why?
- Communicate supervisory expectations about electronic mail to staff members. Do you know the culture of e-mail usage on your campus?

The power of rewards. In some organizations, supervisors do not hold the power to control formal rewards, such as salary and benefits, but there are other types of rewards available to the supervisor, such as positive feedback, public recognition, professional development opportunities, job enrichment, and advancement. Some rewards, however, are not under their control. As an example, consider this new professional's experience:

Where I work, the funds for attending conferences are controlled by a central office administrator other than my supervisor. The person controlling the funds is notorious for approving funds for some staff members, while making others virtually beg for conference funding. It is clear that the best way to get funds for conference travel is to "play up" to the person with the travel budget. I'm not sure if the funds are allocated with a consistent eye for equity. However, most of us feel like the decisions are arbitrary.

Perception is everything. [Conference Coordinator]

In a case such as this, the supervisor can serve as an advocate for staff members in order to save them from the humiliation of having to beg for professional development funds. In a sense, the reward doubles because the individual receives professional development funds and avoids having to beg for them.

The power of access. Having access to individuals and groups with power is another way for new professional supervisors to influence the effectiveness of their staff and to garner the resources they need. The first step is to discover the individuals and groups in the organizations who wield influence in the particular areas of interest to the supervisor (e.g., budgeting, policy-making). Access can then be formal, such as getting appointed to the budget planning committee, or informal, such as establishing a relationship with the chair of the policy and procedures committee.

In addition to information, rewards, and access, other types of power include personality (charisma) and expertise. Being aware of the bases of power in the organization, including one's own, and of ways to utilize them effectively is a major focus of viewing the supervisory role through the political frame.

The power of teams. Regardless of where we work, whether the private or public sector, the value of working collaboratively is well documented. Corbin (2000) shared that, "The power of teamwork remains true today. Multiple people working in unity are so much more powerful than the same number of people working independently" (p. 133). The power of teams could easily be identified as the work of the catalyst or the advocate. Managing the dynamics of a team includes understanding and dealing with multiple personality traits, the varying skill and experience levels, and willingness people have for working collaboratively. Additionally, the conflicts that arise over power and resources within groups make the role of team leader and supervisor particularly challenging. Some groups are easier to mold into teams than others. Corbin (2000) also provides this caution regarding supervising groups of people:

Because of the power of teamwork in organizational success... leaders must arrange workspace for collaborative efforts and arrange the work itself so that each person, when making his or her most expert contribution, produces a necessary part of the whole. Additionally, rewards are given for the team's projects at completion. Ideally, competition is fostered between organizations, not within organizations, which is why rewards are given for individual improvement and not on the basis of comparative performance. The greater reward, however, must be given on a team level- something that can be achieved only through cooperation. (p. 120)

SUPERVISOR AS INTERPRETER

The fourth frame of reference is that of organizational culture. Probably the most elusive of the four frames, it is a significant influence when dealing with campus and personnel issues (see Chapter 2 of this monograph). While organizations can be viewed as machinelike (structural frame), they also have qualities of a culture similar to those of the cultures of racial, ethnic, or religious backgrounds, that is, patterns of shared values, beliefs, assumptions, and symbols. Every organization develops distinctive patterns of beliefs and behaviors over time, many of which are subconscious, that are reflected in myths, stories, rituals, ceremonies, and other symbolic forms. Managers who can interpret and make use of the meaning of symbols have a better chance of influencing their organizations than do those who focus only on the other three frames (Bolman & Deal, 1991).

Institutions of higher education are loaded with very powerful messages about who are members and what they believe. Consider why people cry when they sing the alma mater or why they paint their faces at football games. They do this not because there is a campus policy mandating emotion at football games but because rituals, heroes, and myths are powerful ways to share common meaning and experience within a culture. Faculty, students, alumni, donors, staff, law makers, administrators, parents, and others compete to have their voices heard on campus, but on Saturday afternoon, the crowd, composed of all of these groups, cheers for the football team. It is not accidental that college athletics has symbolic power in higher education.

The cultural frame takes the focus away from what the organization does and how it is done and places emphasis on why we do the things we do, that is, on the meaning of organizational and individual action. The culture of the organization and institution often dictate how supervisors should behave. The *shoulds* that often begin as part of the formal structure become part of the culture. For example, the issue of documentation cited in the section on the structural frame will vary in emphasis and meaning depending on the culture of the particular organization. To the new Assistant Dean, following up a meeting with a memo meant that he was ensuring accurate communication; to his supervisor, it meant that the Assistant Dean did not trust him to do what he said he would do. Formally documenting meetings and agreements was just not part of that organization's culture.

As a supervisor, interpreting and understanding the culture as soon as possible increases chances of staff success. Time in the position helps but so does careful and sensitive observation of practices, reactions, language, and priorities. A new supervisor should observe what people do and listen to the stories they tell about the organization. Who are the departmental heroes and what did they do to gain such fame? What are the rituals of the department? On any campus, one can look around at the department or staff groups that seem to be the tightest knit teams.

What are their special rituals? What are the inside jokes and special stories that made that team seem cohesive? Skilled supervisors learn, over time, how to manage and shape the culture of their staff and of the organization. Practical examples of culture management are special banquets, award ceremonies, regular social gatherings, slogans, t-shirts, songs, and mission statements. One must, however, go beyond the surface meaning of activities to their underlying, more powerful, subconscious meanings. One residence hall director describes the discovery of the cultural meaning of the organization's annual retreat:

Everyone hated going on the annual staff retreat. So I thought. We complained about the heat, and the lack of amenities at the retreat location. The retreat became one of the most talked-about activities of the year. We laughed about the things that happened, and spoke frequently and fondly of the late night conversations and games. But, we all just loved to hate the retreat. When a new director arrived, the retreat was eliminated. You wouldn't believe the amount of complaining we did about the change. The fall just was not the same without the camping trip. It's been years since the last major retreat, but people still tell stories about the people and the events surrounding that trip, even after we left the institution. It became clear that the retreat was the perfect way to bring people together. If nothing else, it was our own folklore.

This retreat was more than just a time for building a team. It was time when organizational stories were passed on to the new generation, a time for people to come together within the context of their mutual discomfort. It was part of the organization's culture. The example gives insight into the importance of rituals and their value beyond the obvious complaints people had about the retreat. If a new supervisor perceives that making a change in one of the department's rituals is necessary, care and caution should be taken. Change often is met with resistance, and change in an organization's culture could mean extraordinary conflict.

In the definition of supervision stated earlier, supervisors do what they do "within the context of an historically based institutional culture." Supervision does not occur in a vacuum. Supervisors need to be aware of the culture of the department as well as the overall organization and the cultures of the various constituency groups within the organization.

INTEGRATING THE FRAMES

That a new supervisor will be a skilled architect, catalyst, advocate, and interpreter in his or her first position is unlikely. He or she will probably be most comfortable and effective with one, perhaps two, of the four frames. Often times organizational setting has a significant impact on the emphasis a supervisor can or will place on one or more of the frames.

One supervisor may be structure-oriented and thrive on budgets, operational calendars, and development of policy and procedures; another may be oriented towards the people in the organization and thrive on collaborative projects, relationships, and committee work. Regardless of how the supervisor is most comfortable, it is wise to practice viewing the organization and a supervisor's role in it through multiple perspectives. The supervisory role requires some skills from each of these perspectives, and focusing solely on one frame will cause important information or action to be missed.

As an example of the need for integrating perspectives, analysis of the typical RA staff meeting serves as a useful scenario. Questions are raised regarding structure (e.g., purpose, agenda, outcomes, degree of formality, required attendance), human resources (e.g., role of RAs, degree of collaboration), and politics (e.g., working together to influence departmental policy). From a cultural perspective, additional questions arise. Why are staff meetings important? Are they weekly rituals that enhance the performance of the group as a whole? Are they weekly requirements to pass along memos from the central administration? Does the group's culture support change, or does the status quo usually prevail? Considering situations from all four of Bolman and Deal's (1991) frames not only raises different questions but also may lead to different outcomes and more effective decisions.

Another common example of the integration of the four frames is the seemingly simple issue of the role of the live-in staff member. One professional shared this story:

When I was a Resident Director (RD), one of the first items on my training agenda was "Please do not contact me in the evening unless there is a building emergency." Well, as it turned out, the previous RD in my building gave his RAs 24-hour access to the key to his apartment, so they could drop by and use the kitchen, watch TV, or just chat. Well, you would not believe how upset my staff became. They really felt as if I had taken away quite a major perk of being an RA. And, they questioned whether or not I really cared about them because I didn't want them to call me after hours.

This RD was not obligated to allow her RA staff to have access to her apartment 24 hours a day. There were, however, ramifications from this change. The students may have associated the apartment and RD access as a reward for being an RA. The veteran RAs passed along to the new RAs the folklore about the conversations they had with their RD while in the apartment in the late evening hours. The new RD took away the reward and, therefore, was perceived as using the power of her position in a negative manner. The RAs translated the removal of the key from the desk as meaning the RD did not care about the RAs or what was happening on the floors. One seemingly reasonable decision quickly became a political and organizational cultural issue.

Turning the Table: Supervisor as Supervisee

Strengths, areas for development, or major skill deficiencies exist in most supervisors, regardless of how many years of experience they have in the profession. What if we find ourselves working with a "bad boss"? It is essential to learn that an extraordinary architect who is not a strong catalyst is probably not a bad boss. Likewise, the supervisor who is a skilled catalyst but a weak architect may also not be a bad boss.

A laundry list of traits that describe a bad boss ought not to be composed of a list of traits that are the opposite of our preferred style of leadership. It is essential to look first for ways to capitalize upon the similarities and differences with our supervisors to the betterment of the organization. Coming from opposite perspectives? Learn how to incorporate a supervisor's perspective in order to enhance personal skills and job effectiveness. Even when differences are extreme, work towards developing a relationship grounded in mutual respect. Once respect between two individuals is established, possibilities for sharing concerns about weaknesses and areas for improvement become more feasible. Learn for ways to accept the differences and learn from them.

There are times when a supervisor's lack of skill or inappropriate behavior warrants concern. A bad supervisor may be someone who is unable to manage job responsibilities. A bad supervisor may have uncivil or unethical behavior. In both cases the subordinate must make some difficult decisions. There are choices to be made in the approach to take when a supervisor's behavior goes beyond a few ineffective skills and starts to seriously and negatively impact the professional and/or personal environment. The sensitive nature of any relationship that has a power and authority differential deserves case-by-case analysis.

The ideal course of action for dealing with conflict is direct confrontation of the problem. If appropriate, confront the supervisor directly with specific issues and requests for behavior change. Use civil language and behavior. If the behavior changes and the outcomes are satisfactory, the story has reached an ideal ending. If the behavior is so extreme that a one-on-one confrontation is troublesome or if the behavior does not change after an initial confrontation, seek out assistance. If mentors are available to help develop a strategy, seek them out for counsel. Additional campus resources include human resources personnel, an ombuds officer, harassment officers, and the direct supervisor of the individual causing concern. Individuals with more experience can lend perspective and strategy to work through difficult situations.

> It is essential to look first for ways to capitalize upon the similarities and differences with our supervisors to the betterment of the organization.

Being a good supervisee. Although this chapter's focus is about the skills of supervision, there is also skill to being a good supervisee. A 25-year veteran of student affairs gave this example from her years providing oversight of the cultural and advocacy programs on her campus:

I supervised a man who had good skills in the specific tasks of the job. However, he confronted without regard to civil behavior and lacked respect for systems and authority. He genuinely believed civility was a euphemism for squelching dissent. He was widely considered untouchable in terms of employee discipline. He has expressed an interest in advancement. With some behavioral changes that have been suggested over the years, he would be an acceptable upper-level professional. I remember one year a friend of mine asked, "What do you think about [name withheld] for our director position?" I had to balance my ethical responsibility to an employee while being responsible in my choice of words to a friend who deserved to know the truth. I simply said that it would be better if I didn't provide a comment in regard to his candidacy. I remember thinking, "I certainly hope I never have anyone say 'no comment' in regard to my candidacy for a job."

We are all well advised to consider that we are a part of larger systems. The choices we make as supervisees are as important as the choices we make as supervisors. There is much discussion on college campuses about civility. Perhaps the lessons of civility statements, like the one paraphrased here from Indiana University of Pennsylvania, are among the most important we can bring to our supervisory relationship. Aside from pursuing excellence in the work that we do and working to meet the expectations of our supervisors and organizations, we can act honestly, take responsibility for our actions, contribute in positive ways to the supervisory relationship and organization, and respect the freedom of all members of the organization to express their point of view. We can seek to be of strong character and integrity. We can discourage and act against intolerance, hatred and injustice, and promote constructive resolution of conflict. We can strive for the betterment of department and university, as well as the world in which we live. A strong work ethic and commitment to civility are a winning combination for a supervisor and supervisee.

CONCLUSION

Understanding and integrating the four frames does not mean that all supervisory decisions will be popular and perfect. Supervisors increase the probability of making a good decision, however, when a deeper organizational understanding informs the decision. Additionally, supervisors may have more empathy with individuals who are opposed to a decision when they see that the opposition is based in a particular way of viewing the situation. Improved decision-making, working relationships, and performance provide ample justification for trying to understand and view the organization through multiple lenses.

One veteran supervisor talked about supervision this way:

I know about the Bolman and Deal model of supervision. We learned it in graduate school. A few years ago I would have called myself the consummate catalyst and a very competent architect/advocate. It is difficult to be a prophet or interpreter in student affairs work until later years; we are so transient. Today, after a few years of attending the "school of hard knocks," I consider myself the consummate realist. My style, any effective supervisor's style, is dependent as much on their own skill as it is on the skill of their personnel and the history and needs of their organization. As I have learned and confronted my own strengths and weakness as a leader, so too have I learned that the key to good supervision is understanding yourself and the organization well enough to make good choices about which perspective or perspectives are most appropriate in any given moment. To me, being the consummate supervisor need not mean being all things to all people in all situations. To me, being the consummate supervisor is getting comfortable with the fact that perfection isn't possible and always striving to be a little better each day.

It is one thing to read about supervision and quite another to actually do it. Each new professional has a unique style that, initially, will be a good fit for some individuals, staffs, and organizations and not such a great fit for others. Strive to weave the principles of lifelong learning, civility, and the perspectives of the architect, catalyst, advocate, and interpreter into your skills as a practitioner.

REFERENCES

Bolman, L. G., & Deal, T. E. (1991). *Reframing organizations: Artistry, choice, and leadership.* San Francisco: Jossey-Bass.

Career Press (1993). *The supervisor's handbook* (2nd Ed.). NY: Author.

Carnegie Foundation for the Advancement of Teaching. (1990). *Campus life: In search of community.* Princeton, NJ: Author.

Carnevale, A. P., & Stone, C. S. (1995). *The American mosaic: An in-depth report on the future of diversity at work.* NY: McGraw Hill.

Corbin, Carolyn. (2000). *Great leaders see the future first: Taking your organization to the top in five revolutionary steps.* Chicago: Dearborn, A Kaplan Professional Company.

Dalton, J. C. (1996). Managing human resources. In S. R. Komives & D. B. Woodard, Jr. (Eds.), *Student Services: A handbook for the profession* (pp. 494-514). San Francisco: Jossey-Bass.

Kaufman, B. E. (1994). *The economics of labor markets.* Fort Worth, TX: The Dryden Press.

Kuh, G. D. (1996). Organizational theory. In S. R. Komives & D. B. Woodard, Jr. (Eds.), *Student services: A handbook for the profession* (pp. 269-294). San Francisco: Jossey-Bass.

Schuh, J. H., & Carlisle, W. (1991). Supervision and evaluation: Selected topics for emerging professionals. In T. K. Miller & R. B. Winston (Eds.), *Administration and leadership in student affairs* (pp. 495-532). Muncie, IN: Accelerated Development.

CHAPTER 5

Collaboration with Academic Affairs and Faculty

CAMILLE CONSOLVO AND MICHAEL DANNELLS

INTRODUCTION

The organizational and functional gap between academic affairs and student affairs is generally distinct and often problematic for student affairs professionals who endeavor to navigate the institution with the ultimate goal of student learning. Collaboration between student affairs professionals and the faculty is one logical and oft-prescribed solution (AAHE, ACPA, & NASPA, 1998; ACPA, 1994, 1999; ACPA & NASPA, 1997).

Collaboration has been defined as working jointly with others in an intellectual endeavor and cooperating with someone with whom one is not immediately connected (Merriam Webster's, 1993). Our intellectual endeavor with faculty is the design and delivery of learning environments and opportunities for students. Because we are not immediately connected with faculty in most institutions, and because faculty tend to see only the formal curriculum as the core of education, we must cross organizational lines and work with faculty to develop a shared vision–a common agenda–for student learning. Working toward this common agenda requires faculty and student affairs professionals to identify and recognize their different assumptions.

UNDERSTANDING BOTH CULTURES

To build bridges between students' in- and out-of-class experiences, new professionals must first understand and appreciate the cultures of both the faculty and student affairs. Although faculty may work at the same institution, they may not necessarily communicate regularly, have common goals, or value undergraduate education in the same way (Eimers, 1999). Faculty tend to identify more with their disciplines than their institution (Love, Kuh, MacKay, & Hardy, 1993). A faculty member's closest colleague may work at another institution. Faculty members are not a homogeneous group, and student affairs professionals must view each faculty member as an individual. To understand the faculty at a particular institution, one must consider the type of institution, the history and traditions of that institution, and the socialization process for faculty.

Despite institutional differences, faculty tend to share four values: 1) a pursuit and dissemination of knowledge; 2) professional autonomy, including academic freedom; 3) collegiality through self-governance; and 4) valuing thinking and reflecting over doing. In contrast, student affairs professionals tend to share four values: 1) an interest in holistic student development; 2) collaboration over autonomy; 3) teamwork; and 4) doing over thinking and reflecting (Love et al., 1993). Understanding both cultures and sets of values facilitates student affairs professionals and faculty working together to create an institutional culture that encourages student learning and development.

In a study of differences among academic disciplines, Braxton and Hargens (1996, in Eimers,1999) suggested that faculty in "soft" sciences (e.g., education, business, humanities) were more likely than faculty in the natural sciences (e.g., math, engineering) to encourage in- and out-of-class contact with students and to create opportunities for students to share their skills and knowledge in the classroom. Thus, student affairs professionals may want to seek out faculty from these fields with whom to collaborate. Again, this will depend on institutional culture and other related variables.

It is essential that, prior to collaboration, new professionals spend significant time learning about their own professional cultures and that of other constituents (Philpott & Strange, in press). This will increase the effectiveness of their working relationships. As one new professional said:

We don't always get much training in how to deal with faculty in our preparation programs. We need to understand it is all about relationships. Faculty are people too.

Another new professional advised:

Take initiative and don't be frustrated with a few isolated pockets of cynicism and disinterest among faculty. Find out each faculty member's niche and how it might fit with your program. It may take many contacts on your part but be patient and persistent, and stay committed.

CONDITIONS FOR COLLABORATION

There are several conditions for effective collaboration (Brown, 1990). Student affairs professionals (new and seasoned) must understand and acknowledge that the mission of colleges and universities—academics—comes first. They must also understand the nature of faculty preparation, priorities, and daily activities. On the academic side, there are certain emerging environmental factors that promote collaboration. Faculty professional development has expanded, and as a result, faculty's conception of their role and obligation to students and their learning has broadened. Broader definitions of scholarship with a focus on teaching and assessment of student outcomes favor collaboration (Banta & Kuh, 1998). Finally, significant numbers of new faculty are joining the academy and may be more open to collaboration, thus increasing possibilities.

Student affairs staff offer expertise in student characteristics, development and learning, program development, supervision, administration, policy development, networking with diverse groups, conflict mediation, and student conduct (Dannells, 1997; Engstrom & Tinto, 1997). This knowledge should be promoted to faculty as an incentive to engage in collaborative efforts.

OPPORTUNITIES FOR COLLABORATION

Brown (1990) described several issues that call for collaboration. These major issues have important implications for how we as student affairs professionals work with our colleagues in academic affairs to improve undergraduate education. With a renewed emphasis on learning, the academic community needs to focus on different methods of teaching and on how to help students learn more effectively. Student affairs professionals can design co-curricular experiences to reinforce course content, identify high-risk classes, and work with instructors to improve success rates, as well as organize discussion groups for students enrolled in common courses. Theme housing, freshman interest groups, living-learning communities, residential communities, and faculty-in-residence programs are excellent examples of how to accomplish these goals.

Curricular reform with a particular emphasis on the general education curriculum is another collaboration opportunity. The liberal education curriculum (e.g., psychology, history, philosophy, the natural sciences, and literature) promotes student development and contributes to the development of identity, competency, autonomy, appreciation for diversity, and the clarification of values. Coupled with a focus on active learning, this general education curricular reform movement provides an opportunity for student affairs professionals to serve as advocates, facilitators, and reinforcers in helping students understand the developmental aspects of the core academic disciplines (Brown, 1990). Some of the methods to achieve these goals are through freshman year integration and transition programs (Banta & Kuh, 1998; Garland & Grace, 1993), incorporating faculty's vocational or career interests into residential life programs (Garland & Grace, 1993), cooperative education/internships, new faculty orientation (Finley, 1996), academic support programs (e.g., study skills labs, writing labs, tutoring), academic advising, honors programs (Brown, 1990), early warning systems for students in academic difficulty, and living-learning communities (Schroeder, 1999).

Gaff (1983) noted that student affairs professionals and other administrative

> Opportunities for collaborative relationships within an institution emerge from the need to focus on different methods of teaching and find ways for students to learn more effectively.

staff should be included in the debates about general education, stating that they "can help set high expectations," and advance learning goals for students outside the classroom. Examples of collaborative ways to accomplish these goals are leadership training (Martin & Murphy, n.d.), service learning (Engstrom & Tinto, 1997; Fried, n.d.), advising student organizations, and facilitating career decisions by connecting academic programs with course and career choices (Garland & Grace, 1993). Other issues that call for collaboration are values education, dealing with diversity issues, and teaching social responsibility (Brown, 1990).

There is a broad range of interactions that occur with some frequency between faculty and student affairs professionals (Brown, 1990), including standing committees or councils, university programs or functions (e.g., admissions, orientation, honors programs, academic support programs), residence halls, health and counseling services, career planning and placement, and student activities and cultural programming. Some other opportunities for interaction and collaboration include campus diversity initiatives and decentralized student services in colleges within a university.

In the past 15 years, many institutions have placed a focus on integrating service learning across the curriculum (Engstrom & Tinto, 1997). Through service learning, students are encouraged to make tangible relationships between classroom content and real-life experiences. Engstrom and Tinto (1997) argued that service learning provides ideal opportunities for collaborative activities between academic and student affairs where both parties can make significant contributions. They cited several institutions that are creatively and effectively forging partnerships in this area.

Banta and Kuh (1998) described outcomes assessment in higher education as "one of the most promising but underused opportunities for collaboration." They argued that it is one of the few activities on campus in which student affairs professionals and faculty can participate equally. New student programs and experiences, as well as co-curricular transcripts, are examples of ways to work collaboratively in the assessment process to focus institutional effort on student learning. Especially at larger, more research-oriented institutions, it may be particularly beneficial for student affairs professionals to demonstrate their ability to collect and analyze outcome data to faculty immersed in research culture.

Table 1 summarizes a variety of deliberate ways in which student affairs professionals can collaborate with their academic colleagues to provide seamless learning environments where students make the most of learning resources that exist both inside and outside of the classroom, and where the curricular and the co-curricular appear to be one whole, continuous experience (ACPA, 1994).

TABLE 1

Opportunities for collaborative efforts between student affairs and academic affairs

- Enrollment management, retention, admissions efforts (Brown, 1990; Martin & Murphy, n.d.)
- Pre-college enrichment courses
- Freshman year integration and transition programs (Fried, n.d.; (Garland & Grace, 1993; Banta & Kuh, 1998)
- Incorporating faculty's vocational or career interests into residential life programs (Garland & Grace, 1993)
- Cooperative education/internships
- Residential life programs: Theme housing, freshman interest groups, living-learning communities, residential communities, faculty-in-residence efforts (Brown, 1990; Martin & Murphy, n.d.; Fried, n.d.; Schroeder, 1999)
- Student discipline (Garland & Grace, 1993; Dannells, 1997)
- Including faculty on unit advisory boards (Brown, 1990)
- Participating in annual week/month events (e.g., Women's History, Alcohol Awareness, Black History)
- Co-curricular transcripts or portfolios (Banta & Kuh, 1998)
- Advising student organizations (Brown, 1990)
- Involvement with student newspaper and/or radio (Brown, 1990)
- Assessment (Banta & Kuh, 1998)
- Study or education abroad
- Serving on faculty governance committees (Brown, 1990)
- University day care centers (Brown, 1990)
- New faculty orientation (Finley, 1996)
- Academic support programs (e.g., study skills labs, writing labs, tutoring) and honors programs (Brown, 1990)
- Faculty development workshops (Finley, 1996)
- Team teaching efforts (Martin & Murphy, n.d.)
- Protection of human subjects committees
- Early warning systems for students in academic difficulty
- Facilitating career decision by making connections between academic programs and course and career choices (Brown, 1990; Garland & Grace, 1993)
- Responding to increased violence/decreased civility on campus (Garland & Grace, 1993)
- Long-range planning groups (e.g., space, resources)
- Joint appointments in student affairs and on the faculty
- Leadership training and coursework on leadership efforts (Martin & Murphy, n.d.)
- Service learning (Engstrom & Tinto, 1997; Fried, n.d.) Serving as consultants for each other

Advice for Building Collaborative Relationships

To build effective relationships, we must assess the environment and identify institutional issues that cross the boundaries between academic affairs and student affairs...

As *The Student Learning Imperative* (ACPA, 1994) implores us, we should attempt to bridge the "functional silos" on campus, make "seamless" what are often perceived by students to be disconnected experiences, and develop collaborative partnerships with faculty and others to enhance student learning. One new professional stated:

We need to reach out more to faculty and make our invitation well known.

To build effective relationships, we must assess the environment and identify institutional issues that cross the boundaries between academic affairs and student affairs (e.g., retention, assessment). We facilitate collaboration by, for example, building relationships with colleagues in learning centers and advising offices that straddle the functional silos, for example, and by developing a shared vision with academic colleagues. By creating cross-functional teams of staff and faculty with diverse skills and experiences, we can understand that faculty are people like ourselves and find ways to connect with them. Persistent attempts to connect with faculty, recognizing them publicly for their collaborative efforts toward student learning, and continually identifying those major issues that lend themselves to collaboration will increase our opportunities to work effectively together. We must leave the comfort and security of organizational boundaries and take some appropriate risks (Schroeder, 1999). One new professional described it this way:

We must educate faculty about what we do and be sensitive to their needs. Listen to them and reach out. However, be "ready to be railed" (challenged) for your efforts. Faculty are paid to think and articulate ideas. Be prepared to help faculty understand our decisions and don't back down, but provide data and information. Don't be defensive, but always do your best to be "even" and a professional, and you will gain their respect.

To do this we should start with small projects to achieve some success and then build on them. We should demonstrate how student affairs programs promote personal and academic development, and engage faculty in discussions about how to make this an outcome of the academic curriculum as well (Brown, 1999).

As student affairs professionals, we need to quit worrying about being second-class citizens and "not getting any respect." One new professional described his experience:

I sometimes think faculty see student activities as the "gym decorators" of the university and our staff as paraprofessionals. To show them otherwise, it is important to be professional and honest, to stand up for the decisions you make, and be proactive and consistent. It's important to be intentional with our programs and services, and serious about our work.

Student affairs professionals should be confident that they make a difference in students' lives and be comfortable living in the breach between being solely a service provider and a faculty member (Hossler, 2001).

Student affairs as a profession must relinquish the weak self-identity that leads to ineffectiveness, an anti-intellectual culture, concern that territory will be gained or lost, and a need to be seen at the center of the institution. Instead, we should begin recognizing the value we have as a service profession while including a focus on learning. We should "transcend real and imagined boundaries, strengthen our identity, and lead effectively from the margins" (NASPA's Think Tank, 2001, p. 2). Right or wrong, initial contacts for collaboration may have to come from student affairs professionals because it is unlikely that most faculty will initiate such contact.

Kuh (1996) suggested several ways to create "seamless" learning environments in collaboration with faculty: invite faculty members to present research findings at student affairs staff meetings, have student life and academic deans, as well as other faculty, attend professional conferences together annually, and hold occasional joint meetings of senior staff. Finley (1996) recommended finding faculty allies who appreciate what student affairs brings to the educational experience, participating in new faculty orientation and following up with these faculty afterward, writing articles for faculty newsletters about services and programs, using brief e-mail messages to keep faculty informed about what is happening in student affairs, and offering to guest lecture in their classes. Helping faculty access students as research participants and serving on institutional review boards for the protection of human subjects is another way of developing faculty allies. As one new professional in student activities suggested:

I started a dialogue with all faculty advisors. The dean of students and I talked with the provost about ways to add some value to faculty merit portfolios through involvement as an advisor. As a result, I have the vice president for student affairs send letters each semester thanking faculty for their service. Faculty want a tangible benefit.

Another new professional in residence life described faculty recognition this way:

I write the president at the end of each year naming faculty that have been involved and their contributions to retention. We make sure that events involving faculty are well publicized on campus so their peers recognize their involvement. We also try to make sure there is a benefit for them. For example, for non-tenured faculty, we talk about possible research and publication opportunities.

New professionals can become engaged by: 1) Getting involved with the academic side of the institution (taking a class, teaching a class, serving on a committee); 2) Getting involved with faculty by collaborating on projects, playing "noon ball," running, or finding other neutral ground in which to establish relationships; 3) Personally inviting faculty to be involved in structured, daytime, time-limited tasks in student affairs (e.g., orientation planning, staff screening and selection, judicial boards); 4) Making faculty experiences comfortable by having some structured segment so faculty know what to expect, providing an escort to introduce them and show them what to do, or having more than one faculty member present; 5) Viewing every interaction as an opportunity to introduce faculty to the values and goals of your unit and the profession; and 6) Following through and having fun (Love et al., 1993). One new professional suggested:

It can be challenging for a faculty member to step out of the familiar (e.g., the classroom) and enter a new environment (e.g., a residence hall) because it is new and can be intimidating. We need to educate them about what we do and escort them into new surroundings.

Often student affairs professionals grouse that they are the ones that always have to approach the faculty and they wish faculty would do the initiating. We need to realize that this is not likely to happen very often, considering faculty culture and values. We must approach faculty to build bridges and create effective learning environments for our students. The key to this involvement is persistence. One new professional described it this way:

It is important to reach out to faculty because the academic mission is central to our mission in student affairs. We must take initiative and not see ourselves as second-class citizens. Some new professionals get frustrated by being the initiators. It is important to look for common ground (e.g., academic expectations, the university as a learning community) and work with faculty from that point.

Although comprehensive research has not been conducted to assess the outcomes of collaboration on student learning, the desired results of improved cognitive, interpersonal, and organizational skills, responsibility for self and community, increased leadership and citizenship, self-understanding, and academic success and retention (Bloland, Stamatakos, & Rogers, 1996) are worth the effort. Persistence, optimism, and understanding with faculty, while maintaining a focus on issues and themes revolving around student learning, will pay big dividends in the end. While historical, organizational, and cultural obstacles may impede easy progress, the greatest barrier to collaboration with faculty, and the one most within our control, is attitude.

REFERENCES

American College Personnel Association (ACPA). (1994). *The student learning imperative: Implications for student affairs.* Washington, DC: Author.

American College Personnel Association (ACPA) and National Association of Student Personnel Administrators (NASPA). (1997). *Principles of good practice for student affairs.* Washington, DC: Authors.

American College Personnel Association (ACPA). (1999). *Higher education trends for the next century: A research agenda for student success.* C. S. Johnson & H. D. Cheatham (Eds.) Washington, DC: Author. http://www.acpa.nche.edu/seniorscholars/trends/trends.htm

American Association for Higher Education (AAHE), American College Personnel Association (ACPA), & National Association of Student Personnel Administrators (NASPA). (1998). *Powerful partnerships: A shared responsibility for learning.* Washington, DC: Authors.

Banta, T. W., & Kuh, G. D. (1998, March-April). A missing link in assessment. *Change, 30,* 40-46.

Bloland, P. A., Stamatakos, L. C., & Rogers, R. R. (1996). Redirecting the role of student affairs to focus on student learning. *Journal of College Student Development, 37,* 217-226.

Brown, R. D. (1999, February). Shaping the future. *ACPA Developments, 25,* pp. 1, 16.

Brown, S. S. (1990). Strengthening ties to academic affairs. In M. J. Barr, M. L. Upcraft, & Associates, *New futures for student affairs,* (pp. 239-269). San Francisco: Jossey-Bass.

Dannells, M. (1997). *From discipline to development: Rethinking student conduct in higher education.* ERIC Higher Education Report, 25(2). Washington, DC: The George Washington University, Graduate School of Education and Human Development.

Eimers, M. T. (1999, March-April). Working with faculty from diverse disciplines. *About Campus, 4,* 18-24.

Engstrom, C. M., & Tinto, V. (1997, July-August). Working together for service learning. *About Campus, 2,* 10-15.

Finley, D. (1996, March). Faculty and student services: Friends or foes. Paper presented at the annual convention of the American College Personnel Association, Baltimore, MD.

Fried, J. (n.d.). *Steps to creative campus collaboration.* NAPSA invited paper. Washington, DC: NASPA.

Gaff, J. G. (1983). *General education today: A critical analysis of controversies, practices, and reforms.* San Francisco: Jossey-Bass.

Garland, P. H., & Grace, T. W. (1993). *New perspectives for student affairs professionals: Evolving realities, responsibilities, and roles.* ASHE-ERIC Higher Education Report, 7. Washington, DC: The George Washington University, Graduate School of Education and Human Development.

Golde, C. M., & Pribbenow, D. A. (2000). Faculty involvement in residential learning communities. *Journal of College Student Development, 41,* 27-40.

Hossler, D. (2001). Reflections on the scholarship of application in student affairs. *Journal of College Student Development, 42,* 356-358.

Kuh, G. D. (1996). Guiding principles for creating seamless learning environments for undergraduates. *Journal of College Student Development, 37,* 135-148.

Love, P., Kuh, G. D., MacKay, K. A., & Hardy, C. M. (1993). Side by side: Faculty and student affairs cultures. In G. D. Kuh (Ed.), *Cultural perspectives in student affairs work* (pp. 37-58). Washington, DC: ACPA.

Martin, J., & Murphy, S. (n.d.). *Building better bridges: Creating effective partnerships between academic affairs and student affairs.* Invited paper. Washington, DC: NASPA.

Merriam Webster's collegiate dictionary (10th ed.). (1993). Springfield, MA: Merriam-Webster.

NASPA's Think Tank. (June, 2001). A challenge to change: A statement on the future of the student affairs profession. Salmon Lake, MT: NASPA.

Philpott, J. L., & Strange, C. (in press). "On the road to Cambridge": A case study of faculty and student affairs in collaboration. *Journal of Higher Education.*

Schroeder, C. C. (1999). Forging educational partnerships that advance student learning. In G. S. Blimling & E. J. Whitt (Eds.), *Good practice in student affairs: Principles to foster student learning,* (pp. 133-156). San Francisco: Jossey-Bass.

CHAPTER 6

Making Professional Connections

LORI M. REESOR

*D*iscussing student involvement on today's college campuses is a common occurrence among student affairs professionals as we constantly search for ways to increase our students' connections to the campus community. Leading authors (Astin, 1984; Astin, 1993; Kuh, Schuh, Whitt, et al., 1991; Rendon, Hope, et al., 1996) have studied this topic in order to help us develop programs and practices that encourage students to be involved and connected. New professionals in student affairs have similar needs for involvement and connection. This chapter provides suggestions for networking with other student affairs professionals and for developing relationships with mentors, as well as recommendations for getting involved in professional organizations.

THE ART OF NETWORKING

Developing a professional network is an important part of professional development. For some, networking has a negative connotation. Many envision the old boy's network, with its connotation of meeting others to gain favors, loyalties, or personal influence (Pancrazio & Gray, 1982). Networking often sounds artificial and manipulative, but it is a means of meeting new colleagues and can be a collaborative, collegial process. Networking can be beneficial for an individual as well as a means for a group to advance. This is particularly true for women or people of color who find support with others outside the dominant group. Networks also enhance a profession by encouraging competence, communication, and support (Pancrazio & Gray, 1982). One description of a network holds that:

> [It] increases the probability of success for its individual members in numerous ways. It acts as an employment service. . . . It gives members useful professional, social, and political contacts, thus expanding their bases of influence. . . . A network also provides members mutually beneficial psychological and eco-

nomic support. . . [A network can also provide] genuineness, empathy, respect or warmth . . . (pp. 16, 17)

Networking is a valuable tool that can be used throughout a career. According to Helfgott (1995), networking skills can help to: "increase your level of confidence; acquire mentors; tap into the 'hidden' job market; exchange valuable information, knowledge, resources, and contacts; give and receive advice and moral support; [and] form long-term personal and professional relationships" (p. 60). As one new professional describes it:

[I think] networking is a process of meeting people, getting to know what they know, and letting them know what you know; exchanging information when it may be beneficial. Networking is important in job searches, research, and in learning about new things.

For the new practitioner, here are some basic suggestions for developing a professional network:

1. *Network at all levels in the organization.* Networking is not just an up/down issue. While there may be value to networking with individuals at higher levels, there are also benefits to developing collegial relationships with peers or counterparts in other areas of the college. For example, if you work in admissions, having contacts in the housing department can assist you in being more successful in your position. Two new professionals share their thoughts about networking:

I find this [networking] easiest when I attend professional functions with another person who already knows many people and is able to introduce me. I find this less intimidating and easier to do. [Admissions Recruiter]

I think an aspect of networking that is often overlooked is peer networking. Most of us think of it as getting to know higher-ups who can help us out. The relationships with colleagues and classmates can be some of the most beneficial networks. [Scholarship Coordinator]

2. *Make it a top priority to seek out colleagues.* If there is an administrator on your campus that you especially respect and would like to get to know, then take the initiative. Ask him or her to join you for a cup of coffee or for lunch. Set up a meeting. It is usually helpful to have a purpose for your meeting beyond building your network. Maybe the person is creating a new program and you would like to learn more about it, or maybe you are thinking about a doctorate one day and want to get his or her opinion. Most administrators have very busy schedules, and while they should welcome the opportunity to get to know new professionals, the meeting should be purposeful. Most administrators and faculty members (even the very busy ones) will be flattered by your

interest and will take the time to meet with you. Examples of networking are shared by two new professionals:

I have realized that in order to network, you must get involved professionally whenever you are offered an opportunity and make yourself known. Attendance is simply not enough—you must actively work at meeting more people, finding similarities between you and others, and keep in touch. [Admissions Staff Member]

I network by learning a little about people I come in contact with, whether that is at a conference, professional activity, or social event. [Financial Aid Counselor]

3. *Be sincere and genuine in your relationships.* If you are trying only to make artificial contacts and use someone, you are not networking. You can tell when someone is fake and only trying to "schmooze"; others can tell, too. "People are quick to recognize and avoid those who are only interested in 'what's in it for me'" (Helfgott, 1995, p. 63). If you are sincerely interested in someone's background, values, thoughts, and opinions, then this is a different type of relationship. Be yourself. Most of us are connected in some way in student affairs or we share mutual friends. Impressions can be long-lasting; be sure they are positive.

4. *Follow up.* Sincere follow-up efforts are the key to turning your network contacts into opportunities (Helfgott, 1995). Send a thank-you note to people who gave you a referral or provided their support. Be prepared to develop other contacts in order to keep the relationship going. A one-time encounter is not networking. For some individuals, it takes a number of interactions before they start to get to know you and consider you part of their network. Do not be discouraged if you meet someone a dozen times and they still do not remember who you are. This happens to all of us; do not take it personally. It just means you may not develop a significant relationship with that person.

Networking is an important skill in developing relationships within your institution, with colleagues at other colleges or universities, and in professional organizations. A residence hall director observes that "I have found that networking is the key to finding a job, and the resources you develop can prove invaluable later in life."

MENTORING

Finding a Mentor
As with networking, various definitions exist for mentor. For purposes of this chapter, the following definition was adapted from Moore and Salimbene (1981): a mentor is a more experienced professional who guides, advises, and assists in numerous ways the career of a less experienced, often younger,

upwardly mobile protégé in the context of a close professionally-centered relationship usually lasting one year or more.

Many research studies (Bell, 1996; Burke, 1984; Caruso, 1992; Kelly, 1984; Kogler Hill, Bahniuk, Dobos, & Rouner, 1989; Kram, 1985) show that mentors can have a positive impact on individuals' careers. In fact, some studies show that those who experience supportive behavior such as mentoring have more opportunities for success, advancement, or achievement in their careers (Kogler Hill, et al., 1989; Wunsch, 1994). The profession of student affairs is no different. Many of us learn early on that mentoring is an important part of our career development. The question is how to develop mentoring relationships.

Networking can be an important factor or step in the initiation process of meeting a mentor (Helfgott, 1995; Kelly, 1984). In one research study, student affairs professionals suggested that new professionals take a proactive approach in initiating relationships with a mentor (Kelly, 1984). Many new professionals believe that the senior student affairs administrator taps his or her magic wand and deems one new professional the protégé. Rarely does it occur this way. Often, it is the responsibility of the new professionals to initiate the relationship.

Kelly (1984) recommends that, to begin the mentoring process, you first assess your own needs: what do you want from a mentor, what kind of help do you need, and who can provide it to you? Typically, you can expect a mentor to provide emotional support and direct assistance with professional and career development and to act as a role model (Tentoni, 1995). It is also appropriate to want different things from mentors. Once you determine your needs, ask other colleagues to identify potentially good mentors. Create and take advantage of opportunities to interact. Put yourself in situations that allow you to be highly visible and always do a good job at whatever you are doing (Kelly, 1984). This is how a few new professionals met their mentors:

When I first started my new position at the college, I knew the vice president was involved in our professional association. I made an appointment to talk with him about ways I could get involved. Little did I know that he would ask me to assist him with a national task force. This was the start of our mentoring relationship. [Residence Hall Director]

I find someone with whom I agree in their management or professional work style and I try to build a relationship with this person in order to learn more about how he or she became successful. [Admissions Recruiter]

I found a mentor by attending a conference and hearing a speaker. I really understood and liked her ideas and thought I could learn from her. So I approached her and introduced myself a couple of times and then asked to work for her for free [as an intern]—anything to work for someone who could teach me something new. [Admissions Supervisor]

Kelly (1984) provides an excellent list of characteristics to look for in a potential mentor: a similar or shared value system, time availability, professional competence in the area where you desire expertise, an active contributor to the field, a genuine interest in your professional development (a nurturing personality), someone you trust, an open communicator, and someone you like (p. 53).

Fortunately, these characteristics vary among individuals, which means plenty of opportunities exist to select different mentors. "Effective mentors are like friends in that their goal is to create a safe context for growth. They are also like family in that their focus is to offer an unconditional, faithful acceptance of the protégé" (Bell, 1996, p. 7).

It is important to realize that selecting a mentor takes time, effort, and commitment, so be patient if a relationship takes a while to develop. The ideal is to have a number of mentors with different expectations to challenge and support you. As Batchelor states (1993, p. 381), "Mentoring relationships often develop into rich and helpful lifelong friendships." You will receive many rewards, as two professionals attest:

The benefit [of having a mentor] is having advice and concern from an individual who has already traveled down the career road you are traveling. [Financial Aid Counselor]

I see many benefits to mentor relationships—it is a great way to learn about new jobs; you can learn from others' experiences; you have a person with whom you can discuss important work issues with the assumption that they may have greater insight into the problem; and it overall produces a more positive work environment because mentors enjoy their status (I am assuming) and they enjoy the chance to help develop a new professional. [Admissions Recruiter]

Challenges with Mentors

Successful mentorships are mutually beneficial not only for the individuals involved but for the organization (Rosenbach, 1993; Sandler, 1993). At the same time, as with any relationship, it takes two individuals to make it work. Both individuals need to cultivate the relationship. Adapted from Trimble's (1994) suggestions for protégés, here are a few recommendations to make the most of the relationship with your mentor:

1. *Clarify needs and expectations.* It is important to acknowledge that your mentor has certain strengths and will not be able to meet every one of your needs. By matching your needs with the mentor's strengths, you should both feel more successful in the relationship.

2. *Be time-conscious.* Most mentors are busy, and while they may value the relationship, be respectful of their schedules. Set up appointments in advance and have a specific purpose when you meet. Do not become a burden on your mentor.

3. *Create a dialogue.* With any relationship, it is important to know when to stop talking and when to be a good listener. Ask for clarification when needed. Seek to understand the values and reasons for decisions. Ask mentors to share their experiences that may help you understand your own situation. Creating give-and-take communication challenges both of you and helps you gain new insights and discoveries.

4. *Foster respect and appreciation for a valued professional.* As a protégé, you are seeking someone to support and care for you and your career. Show the same interest and care for your mentor. A caring attitude is important in the mentor relationship. Provide the mentor with positive feedback. This can occur in many forms, whether it be a personal note, nominating him or her for an award, or just saying thank you. One residence hall director showed appreciation for her mentor in this way:

> ***One of my mentors had started a new job at a different campus. I sent her a card during her first week to let her know that even though we were not in the same location anymore, I still thought of her.***

Cross-Race and Cross-Gender Mentors

As mentioned earlier, it is ideal to develop mentor relationships that meet your different needs. The most common relationship tends to be with members of the same gender and race (Kelly, 1984). In addition, much has been written about the importance and challenges of mentoring for women and professionals of color (Batchelor, 1993; Burke, 1984; Hawks & Muha, 1991; Kelly, 1984; Kram, 1985; Luebkemann & Clemens, 1994; Smith & Davidson, 1992). Since most top administrators are white males, mentoring can assist in the professional development of underrepresented groups. Some challenges can also exist with mentors who are culturally different from their protégés.

Much literature exists on the potential problems of cross-gender mentoring relationships. At times, men and women may assume more stereotypical roles in relating to each other (Kram, 1985; Rosenbach, 1993). One new professional said, "I greatly respect my mentor but at times he acts like my father as opposed to my professional advisor." In issues related to gender or sexual orientation, as significant relationships develop, increasing intimacy and sexual tensions can result. "A more frequent disadvantage for women being mentored by men are the innuendoes about the relationship from people who find it hard to believe that any relationship between a man and woman is not sexual" (Sandler, 1993, p. B3). Develop appropriate boundaries so that the intentions of the relationship are clear. As with any potential sexual harassment situation, "the dangers in the traditional mentoring model are not necessarily gender-related, but rather are a function of the imbalance of power within the relationship" (Johnsrud, 1991, p. 9).

For new professionals of color working in predominantly white institutions, there may be a need to connect with individuals from similar backgrounds or cultures. Ideally, it is helpful to find support within student affairs. In some institutions, however, finding other professionals of color may be difficult. Regardless of the support found in your own department or division, your institution may have other support groups or networks available. Many campuses have a Hispanic network or an African American faculty and staff council. These organizations can help you meet other staff members on campus who may share common experiences. If groups like this do not exist, this may be your opportunity to create one. You may also need to look outside your institution to community or civic organizations, or even colleagues at other institutions. There may be some statewide networks or groups that you could join. Regardless of which avenue you choose, it is important to develop relationships.

When I first came to campus, I made contact with the Office of Multicultural Affairs. Through that office, I learned of the African American Network. This group of faculty, professional staff, and support staff met monthly at a local restaurant. We also had a listserv so we could communicate through e-mail. It was a way for me to feel connected with others and learn about special cultural opportunities. [Multicultural Advisor]

The literature relating to cross-racial mentoring is more limited. The benefits of same-race mentoring include: a) the ability to discover similarities rather than emphasizing differences; and b) the exhibition of cultural sensitivity (Luna & Cullen, 1995). Some research shows that cross-race mentoring relationships have not been as successful because of organizational and personal barriers (Luna & Cullen, 1995; Rosenbach, 1993). Because socializing and informal activities are often involved in mentoring, there may be pressure to participate only with individuals from a similar background. Cultural differences may lead to misinterpretations, but Rosenbach (1993) argues that "racism and sexism in the workplace will disappear as leaders learn to work in diverse teams and begin to view all members as friends and colleagues" (p. 148). Therefore, it is recommended that mentor relationships cross gender and ethnic lines to enhance learning opportunities and improve overall organizational climate (Luna & Cullen, 1995; Rosenbach, 1993; Sandler, 1993).

Stages of Mentoring

Johnsrud (1991) describes a developmental process common to the relationship between mentors and protégés. In the early stages, the relationship tends to be more dependent. The protégés may rely more on guidance from the mentor and have a strong desire to please the mentor. Protégés may need more confirmation. As protégés move on to the independent stage, they are more likely to establish their purpose as distinct from the mentor. They may ask questions such as: "Am I competent and independent if I am still being helped?" "Will I always be a protégé?" At the interdependent stage, "persons have the ability to fulfill for one another the yearning for connectedness and the yearning for identity" (Johnsrud, 1991, p. 15).

Working through developmental stages with a mentor is a normal process. Just as our parents will always see us as children, mentors often see us always as their protégés. It is not uncommon to outgrow mentors or to disagree or have ethical conflicts with them. Mentors are not perfect; they are human beings and make mistakes. They may disappoint you. They may give you bad advice. At these times, reassess your needs and their strengths, and determine realistic expectations of the relationship.

While mentors can provide challenges, most of the time they provide mutually beneficial and caring relationships. By having numerous mentors, you have the opportunity to receive many perspectives on complex issues. One residence hall coordinator states,

Every time I am contemplating a major issue related to my career, I touch base with all my mentors. Each one provides a different angle and perspective that I may not have thought of. I value all of their thoughts.

Mentoring relationships take time, effort, and work. The result can be long-lasting, meaningful relationships that allow you to grow and develop as a person and professional. "With a supportive environment and the right attitude, mentoring can be a powerful force to empower followers to be leaders" (Rosenbach, 1993, p. 149).

GETTING INVOLVED IN PROFESSIONAL ASSOCIATIONS

A common question asked by new professionals is: "Should I get involved in professional organizations?" The answer is a resounding "yes!" and the reasons are many (Nuss, 1993). Networking and seeking out mentors are two ways of developing professional connections, but professional organizations provide learning experiences different from those obtained on one's own campus. They allow for observing leadership styles in a different venue. Further, they are ways to connect with other professionals who share similar interests. For many, being involved in professional organizations involves a "sense of obligation to help advance the status of the profession and fund programs that assist it" (Nuss, 1993, p. 368). Professional organizations can also be a way to develop new friendships, networks, and mentors. One new professional described her involvement:

I have become involved in professional organizations by meeting others within my field, developing friendships, and then volunteering to serve on committees with these other professionals. This has been a great way to learn more about my field and other organizations and to grow professionally. [Admissions Supervisor]

Preparing on the Home Front

This section presents various ways of getting involved in professional organizations. It does not tell you which ones to join or which ones are the best. A listing of the best-known student affairs associations is provided in Appendix A. Read through this list and then talk to your colleagues, faculty, mentors, and network about the history, organizational structure, culture, and purpose of the organizations in which you are interested. You may want to take advantage of the information available by reading the professional associations' web sites. Again, discuss with your supervisor his or her expectations or support for certain organizations.

Before you rush out to join a number of professional organizations and get involved with one or more of them, it is crucial you make sure things are in place in your job and on your campus. This means consulting with your supervisor about his or her thoughts on and support for professional involvement. Support might include financial contributions for attending conferences or meetings; it might mean support to take time off work (and not use vacation time); it could be using office supplies (postage costs, phone calls, etc.) to assist in your professional development.

One example of this kind of supervisory consultation is reflected in a conversation between a hall director and the housing director about getting involved in the American College Personnel Association (ACPA). The housing director felt this was inappropriate for the hall director but was supportive of the person getting involved in the Association of Colleges and University Residence Halls Officers-International (ACUHO-I). It is common for new professionals to receive some funding for a regional conference, but national conferences might have to be paid out of your own personal budget. Sometimes this policy differs if you are presenting a program. All of these things are important to clarify in advance so that your supervisor is supportive of your involvement and you are aware of the parameters before you become involved. The bottom line is, you were hired to perform the duties and responsibilities of your job. After you are performing those to your fullest ability and meeting the expectations of your supervisor, then you are ready to get more involved in professional associations.

Making the Most Out of Professional Conferences

Attending conferences is one way of getting involved in professional organizations. It is an effective way to learn more about what the organization has to offer, its members, and future opportunities. For new professionals, it might be advantageous to start by attending a state or regional conference. These events are usually smaller, allowing for more personal connections and easier navigation. No matter what your position is (whether you are a new professional or mid-level manager), being a newcomer to a conference can be intimidating.

There is a sense that everyone already knows one another and you are the outsider. Be careful before you make quick judgments about the friendliness or openness of an organization based on your initial observations. Student affairs professionals are rarely exclusionary. What may seem like a clique is really a group of friends and colleagues who have known one another for years and are getting together for their annual event. One new professional described his first conference this way:

I had just arrived at the hotel, tired because the plane was late and it took longer than I had thought to arrange for transportation. I immediately felt like a new freshman on campus trying to find the registration area. Once I asked for directions several times, I found the area only to notice several small groups of people talking. I wondered if anyone would ever talk to me. Then someone shouted my name and it was a good friend from grad school. I realized that I, too, knew people here and it would be okay. [Residence Hall Director]

There are some important tips that can be followed for making the most of your first (or second or third) professional conference (Swanson, 1996):

1. *Attend the session designed for newcomers or first-time attendees.* This session provides helpful information regarding the conference and the organization. Often, you will have an opportunity to meet some of the leaders of the organization. You will also meet other newcomers so that you can begin your own network at the conference.

2. *Attend as many keynote speeches and interest sessions as possible.* Once you receive your conference program guide, review it carefully and mark the sessions you would like to attend. Select two or three options for each session time block as some sessions may be closed when you arrive. If you are with other staff members from your institution, split up and get to as many different sessions as you can. Arrive early at sessions because some fill up quickly. Go to the opening session and reception. This helps you get a sense of the conference, the association, and the leadership.

3. *Meet new people.* Introduce yourself to people around you. Contacts are one of the greatest benefits of the conference. You will be amazed at the smallness of the world of student affairs. If you do meet someone with whom you would like to stay connected, exchange business cards. Visit as many university-sponsored receptions as you can. You will meet a lot of people there and can learn how to get more involved. You could even end up with a full meal, which is important given the low budgets of new professionals. Attend task force or commission meetings.

4. *Attend business meetings.* This is an opportunity to learn more about network, commission, or regional activities. While business meetings sound formal

and only for those who have invitations, you will find that most business meetings are open to all members. Again, these activities are a great time to volunteer and get involved. Also, by attending your state or regional business meetings, you will learn more about the professional development activities happening closer to home.

5. *Enjoy the time away.* Treat yourself to some fun and excitement. Use your free time and meals to get to know others and share ideas. If special tours or events are offered, try to take advantage of them. While financial limitations may be restricting, often a low-cost activity is provided. If you are visiting a new area, try to visit some of the local highlights. Seeing new places is a perk of attending conferences—take advantage of the opportunity. Not all learning occurs in the interest sessions.

6. *Reflect on the experience.* When the conference is over and you return to campus, it is natural to feel exhausted and exhilarated. Focus on what you learned. Share the information and handouts with your colleagues. Follow up on the contacts you made at the conference by sending a short note. Thank your supervisor again for the opportunity to attend.

Levels of Organizational Involvement

Throughout your career, your interest in certain organizations may vary. Some new professionals maintain constant membership in a more general association like NASPA or ACPA and then, depending upon their specific job responsibilities, they may join a more specialized interest organization (Nuss, 1993). Once you determine which organization is most interesting to you, it is possible to become involved at various levels (Nuss, 1993).

1. *Being a passive member or consumer.* At this stage you are an official member but may only receive the mailings or documents to stay current in the profession. You may want to take advantage of some of the technological services provided by many organizations, i.e., joining a listserv. At some point you may start attending the state, regional, or national conferences but you still feel more like an observer or spectator. You may want to consider joining one of the committees or special interest groups. For example, NASPA has a New Professionals Knowledge Community; other organizations may have a Black Caucus. Some professional organizations also have electronic learning communities, which allow you to develop connections and gain new knowledge through use of technology. These organizations are effective ways to connect with other professionals with similar interests.

Once you are ready to increase your involvement in the association, there are a number of steps you can take. The first is to start volunteering at the conference. This is an excellent way to meet other people and start learning more about the real workings of the operation. When you attend the conferences, be sure to go to the business meetings and socials. These events provide ways for you to meet the leaders of the organization and hear about the current activities and events. At almost every business meeting, officers will ask for volunteers to help with future programs. This is your chance to get involved.

2. *Becoming a contributor.* Another way to be involved in the professional association is as a contributor (Nuss, 1993). This could involve writing a proposal to present a program, writing an article for the newsletter, or submitting research results for publication. If you are interested in presenting a program, talk with others who have had program proposals accepted. Ask to see a copy of their proposal so you get an idea of how to complete one. Ask a mentor or active member in the organization to review your proposal and give you feedback. Ask one of your mentors to help you present. This is a great way to continue that relationship and become more involved.

3. *Serving as a coordinator.* This means you are responsible for planning, coordinating, or directing efforts of other volunteers (Nuss, 1993). Typically, this responsibility is on a state, regional, or national level and often requires a time commitment of six months to two years. You will likely be working with volunteers all over the country, which could involve interaction by phone, e-mail, or regular mail. Coordinators need good skills in coordinating, budgeting, and supervising, as well as strong interpersonal and communication skills (Nuss, 1993). The expectations for volunteers in professional associations are no different than those for employees. Be thorough, dependable, responsible, and effective. Although you are working for a volunteer association, the accountability and expectations of high quality are no less than for your paid position.

4. *Holding an officer position.* The highest level of involvement is governance (Nuss, 1993). This means being elected or appointed to a regional or national board. At this level, individuals affect policy and long-term planning for the organization. The time commitment can be significant. While this is not a typical level in which new professionals participate, it is appropriate to set goals and plans for reaching this stage at some point in your career.

So where do you start in this area of professional involvement? As always, it starts with a self assessment. What do you hope to accomplish? What talents do you have? How can you contribute? What are some areas you wish to develop? Once you have your own goals, let your mentors know of your plans. Have them introduce you to the leaders of the association as a means of certification of your talents. When you meet the leaders, instead of simply saying, "I want to get involved," tell them some of the specific things you would like to do. When you can, follow up in writing and include a resume so that the leader or decision maker can know how to best apply your talents and skills. Following up with an e-mail is also useful. Finally, if it does not happen the first time, try again. Many leaders receive a lot of communication from their professional associations (as well as their own work), so be patient and contact them again if you do not hear from them right away.

Professional associations play an important role in your career. The benefits include meeting valued colleagues and making friendships, learning about campus issues from new perspectives, and having access to cutting-edge research documents and vital federal, state, and local updates related to students and higher education. Once you become involved, you have an opportunity to establish a professional reputation beyond your campus. Lastly, you can influence the future of the profession. The rewards are great and the expectation is that you should be professionally involved, nothing less.

CONCLUSION

One out of three new professionals leaves student affairs every year (Woodard & Komives, 1990). This is a disadvantage to the professionals as well as to the specific campuses. One way for new professionals to remain in the profession is to develop connections. These connections can occur through networking, mentor relationships, and involvement in professional associations. It is up to you to begin this process. While it takes time and effort, the personal and professional benefits are worthwhile.

REFERENCES

Astin, A. W. (1984). Student involvement: A developmental theory for higher education, *Journal of College Student Personnel, 24,* 297-308.

Astin, A. W. (1993). *What matters in college.* San Francisco: Jossey-Bass.

Batchelor, S. W. (1993). Mentoring and self-directed learning. In M. Barr (Ed.), *The handbook of student affairs administration* (pp. 378-389). San Francisco: Jossey-Bass.

Bell, C. R. (1996). *Managers as mentors: Building partners for learning.* San Francisco: Berrett-Koehler.

Burke, R. J. (1984). Mentor in organizations. *Group & Organization Studies, 9,* 353-372.

Caruso, R. E. (1992). *Mentoring and the business environment: Asset or liability?* Brookfield, VT: Dartmouth.

Hawks, B. K., & Muha, D. (1991). Facilitating the career development of minorities: Doing it differently this time. *The Career Development Quarterly, 39,* 251-260.

Helfgott, D. (1995). Take 6 steps to networking success. *Planning Job Choices: 1995.* Bethlehem, PA: College Placement Council.

Johnsrud, L. K. (1991). Mentoring between academic women: The capacity for interdependence. *Initiatives, 54*(3), 7-17.

Kelly, K. E. (1984). Initiating a relationship with a mentor in student affairs: A research study. *NASPA Journal, 21,* 49-54.

Kogler Hill, S. E., Bahniuk, M. H., Dobos, J., & Rouner, D. (1989). Mentoring and other communication support in the academic setting. *Group & Organization Studies, 14,* 355-368.

Kram, K. E. (1985). *Mentoring at work: Developmental relationships in organizational life.* Glenview, IL: Scott, Foresman.

Kuh, G. D., Schuh, J. H., Whitt, E. J., & Associates (1991). *Involving colleges.* San Francisco: Jossey-Bass.

Luebkemann, H., & Clemens, J. (February, 1994). Mentors for women entering administration: A program that works. *National Association of Secondary School Principals Bulletin, 78,* 42-45.

Luna, G., & Cullen, D. L. (1995). *Empowering the faculty: Mentoring redirected and renewed* (ASHE-ERIC Higher Education Report, No. 3). Washington, DC: Association for the Study of Higher Education.

Moore, K. M., & Salimbene, A. M. (1981). The dynamics of the mentor-protégé relationships in developing women as academic leaders. *Journal for Educational Equity and Leadership, 2*(1), 51-64.

Nuss, E. M. (1993). The role of professional associations. In M. Barr (Ed.), *The handbook of student affairs administration* (pp. 364-377). San Francisco: Jossey-Bass.

Pancrazio, S. B., & Gray, R. G. (1982). Networking for professional women: A collegial model. *Journal of NAWDAC, 45,* 16-19.

Rendon, L. I., Hope. R. O., & Associates. (1996). *Educating a new majority: Transforming America's educational system for diversity.* San Francisco: Jossey-Bass.

Rosenbach, W. E. (1993). Mentoring: Empowering followers to be leaders. In W. E. Rosenbach & R. L. Taylor (Eds.), *Contemporary issues in leadership* (pp. 141-151). Boulder, CO: Westview.

Sandler, B. R. (March 10, 1993). Women as mentors: Myths and commandments. *The Chronicle of Higher Education,* p. B3.

Smith, E.P., & Davidson, W. S., (1992). Mentoring and the development of African American graduate students. *Journal of College Student Development, 33,* 531-539.

Swanson, R. M. (1996). *How to do a conference?* [brochure] Washington, DC: American Association of Collegiate Registrars and Admissions Officers.

Tentoni, S. C. (1995). The mentoring of counseling students: A concept in search of a paradigm. *Counselor Education and Supervision, 35,* 32-42.

Trimble, S. (February, 1994). A protégé's guide to mentoring. *National Association of Secondary School Principals Bulletin, 78,* 46-48.

Woodward, D. B., & Komives, S. R. (1990). Ensuring staff competence. In M. Barr and M. L. Upcraft (Eds.), *New futures for student affairs* (pp. 217-238). San Francisco: Jossey-Bass.

Wunsch, M. A. (1994). Giving structure to experience: Mentoring strategies for women faculty. *Initiatives, 56*(1), 1-10.

CHAPTER 7

Reconciling Life and Work for the New Student Affairs Professional

J. DOUGLAS TOMA AND KELLY A. GRADY

*A*t carnivals . . . there is a man who spins plates on top of various poles. . . . The plate spinner gives one plate a vigorous spin and moves on to the second. As he walks back and forth across the stage, he amazes the audience with the number of plates he is able to keep up and spinning. (Ashford, 1996, p. 121)

Student affairs professionals are also carnival plate spinners of a sort. They work very hard to keep a number of plates spinning—professional plates and personal ones—in order to both impress the audience (multiple audiences, actually) and avoid shattering any plate. Over time, new professionals become increasingly efficient at their task. At some point, however, they recognize that they can only keep so many plates atop so many poles. They also discover that the plate spinning demonstration only works when they find a balance between the number of personal plates and professional plates spinning at one time.

Indeed, the necessary accommodation of the personal and the professional is commonly framed in terms of balance. For the new student affairs professional, as for other more experienced professionals, finding such a balance is often difficult but essential. This chapter examines the ongoing goal of attaining a healthy equilibrium between work life and personal life for individual student affairs professionals. The issue of work-life balance in its broader societal context is explored. In addition to reviewing current thought on reconciling the personal and the professional, we include the voices of several new student affairs professionals. They reflect upon their attempts to sort through the issues of an overly enriched work life, of evaluation and self-evaluation, and of upward career mobility.

The concept of balance in our society is examined by asking two central questions. The first question is: What really is the goal here? This question raises several others, of course. Is the goal to find a balance between work and life that allows new professionals to pursue both fully? Can one ever really have it all? Are new professionals—or any professionals—asking too much of themselves in their desire for balance? Is balance an achievable or even desirable goal? The second major question is more straightforward: If balance is the end, why does it seem so hard to reach? The pursuit of efficiency and balance is examined. Certainly skills can be improved, creating more time, but balance ultimately comes down to making choices based on values. Is it possible to choose both career and wellness?

The conclusion offers several lessons based on the quest for balance. Our *a priori* assumption is that finding a balance between work and life is more complicated than applying some simple time management tips. It requires that new professionals step back and truly examine their lives. Finding something even approaching a satisfying or comfortable balance demands that new professionals come to appreciate the culture in which they work and continually assess their fit within that culture. It also requires that they consider their career stage, as well as where they hope to go and how much getting there will cost. The potential reward for the new professional is an exciting and fulfilling journey.[1]

UNDERSTANDING THE SOCIETAL CONTEXT

It is a common struggle to find balance, exacerbated to the extent people feel that they are failing in one of their multiple roles as partners, workers, parents, friends, or citizens (Reich, 2002). The personal nature of these dilemmas makes it easy to overlook the pervasive societal factors of a new economy, which make achieving balance more difficult than in the past (Reich, 2002). The self-help literature asserts that balance is within our reach if we become more efficient, make choices, and establish boundaries. While these texts provide specific tools with varying degrees of success, they oversimplify the problem of balance, presenting it as an individual one without notice of the societal context.

In *The Future of Success,* Robert Reich (2002) explains the new economy as the era of the "great deal." As consumers, there are benefits, as it is easier than ever to find the exact product at the desired price. On the other side, as workers, competition is fiercer, demanding cheaper and better products, faster. Workers in the higher education industry are not immune to these pressures:

Fiercer competition has spread to nonprofit institutions as well. Even the stuffiest, most hidebound universities, hospitals, museums, and charities must now innovate, because they're subject to the same underlying dynamic that's affecting the rest of the economy. Attendees, patrons, and donors have an increasingly wider choice from which to pick, better information about how

---

[1] In referring to work, the research literature is consistent in categorizing it as paid work. In referring to life outside of work, terms such as family and personal time are used. These terms are inclusive of single and partnered people and those who have children or other extended family. We use these terms in these ways and, when findings are specific to a qualified group, they are so noted.

each institution is performing, and greater capacity to switch to one that satisfies them more. So nonprofits have to be better, faster, and cheaper, too. (Reich, 2002, p. 32)

Organizations, and therefore employees, must hustle just to maintain. There seems to be no slow track running parallel to the fast track—an employee is innovative and contributing, or that employee is unemployed.

The new economy provides important additional benefits besides consumption. Skills are increasingly said to matter rather than position—and opportunities with lucrative rewards are often abundant for those with the right skills. The new economy has created seemingly not only more choices but also more seductive choices. The marginal cost for turning down an opportunity can be significant in terms of career or finances and in many cases it simply cannot be refused.

As a result, people are working harder and jobs are less stable. Americans are working more hours than they did in 1990 and more than any other industrialized country (International Labour Organization, 2002). It is not just time physically at work, but it is a blending of work and home. Physical boundaries of the past mean little in a digital age permeable by e-mail, Internet files, cell phones, and beepers (Bollier & Firestone, 1997). Business is running 24/7, and Americans do not want to lose their competitive edge. Further, customers—and in the case of student affairs, students—increasingly want their needs addressed around the clock. The result for many new professionals can be a sense that they have lost balance—that work has surrounded them and is poised to subsume their lives.

BALANCE AND EFFICIENCY

This goal of balance is often described dualistically—work versus life or career versus family—when in fact work and personal life are interdependent. Success in one area enhances the other, and the reverse is true as well (Freidman & Greenhaus, 2000). In itself, work is not the problem. The right job improves self-esteem, satisfaction with self-growth, and health (Reich, 2002). What can cause problems is the psychological spillover of being occupied by thoughts and worry of work when engaged in other activities. Quite logically, when psychological involvement in work detracts from involvement outside of work, it is likely that a professional is less satisfied with his or her personal life (Friedman & Greenhaus, 2000).

The metaphor of balance seems to be a constant in any discussion of finding ways to accommodate the right amount of work time and personal time. Kofodimos (1993) defines this balance as "finding the allocation of time and energy that fits your values and needs, making conscious choices about how to structure your life, and integrating inner needs and outer demands" (p. 8). Advice abounds on identifying a satisfying balance and how to get there. A visit to the bookstore or the public library yields many books filled with ideas about how to

> **[The] goal of balance is often described dualistically—work versus life or career versus family—when in fact work and personal life are interdependent.**

rethink your life in order to find an appropriate balance between office and home.

A well-developed scholarly literature on work-life issues also exists. Caproni (1997) suggests that organizational theorists "seem determined to identify what the work-life balance is (or should be), applaud its benefits for individuals and organizations, and offer individual and organizational prescriptions for achieving balance" (p. 47). The problem of finding balance is a common one among professionals—and adjusting to a new job, perhaps a new location and new peer group as well, can complicate the goal for new professionals in student affairs. The fact that the profession is built on an ethic of service, where major responsibilities involve responding to students at unpredictable times, makes the need for balance even more compelling.

Typically, the balance that new professionals desire is treated mainly as a matter of increasing efficiency. However, there are only so many hours and numerous tasks to accomplish, and the work involves high stakes. Student affairs professionals too frequently mirror many other groups in a belief that success as a person is measured, in large part, by productivity at work. Still, their personal life is also important to them. New professionals want to succeed at both, but their desire begs an important question: how can they do it all?

On the surface, the question has a rather direct two-part answer: find more hours in the day or make fewer commitments. New professionals become more efficient as they become more experienced and apply lessons learned, of course. What is more challenging, however, is finding time to reflect and learn in more intentional ways. This is especially true in the context of the consistent wave of urgent matters that confront any student affairs professional that can have more immediate resolution than addressing the complex and nebulous challenges associated with the life-work equation.

Moreover, skill building and improved efficiency have their limits. They are compelling because the assumption is that new professionals can do it all and still have it all, even when it seems that they are already so stretched. All people have to do is become smarter (so the books tell them) at doing what is expected of them or what they expect of themselves. Jackson (1996) suggests why efficiency is such a powerful notion and warns that efficiency alone is not a cure all:

Unfortunately, the external markers of success—which reflect the satisfaction of others regarding our performance—may not translate into feelings of personal satisfaction. Searching for more and better ways to work efficiently is, I think, a strategy built on the implicit assumption that accomplishing more will lead to more recognition from others and, therefore, more personal satisfaction. . . . This logic is flawed. . . . There are, after all, human limits to how much one can accomplish—incremental gains in efficiency and its associated rewards (internal as well as external ones) become harder to achieve as one becomes more efficient and productive. (p. 354)

Further, the theory of efficiency ignores the emerging reality of the new economy that responsibilities and opportunities at work do not remain stable. Once responsibilities are mastered, new "duties as assigned" fill the gaps. Those interested in career growth often choose to pursue and accept new projects that add to their responsibilities.

New professionals may also run the risk of becoming so hyper-efficient that they alienate others, choosing task completion over the interpersonal relationships that are a valued part of a student affairs staff. They may even distance the friends and family for whom, presumably, they are becoming more efficient in order to share time. In short, efficiency, when it becomes the central value in life, has a tendency to spill over into other parts of life where it has no real value and may even be a problem (Kofodimos, 1997).

The second part of the answer—committing to doing fewer things—causes professionals to attempt to manage their overall workload. Anyone who works with college students knows that the job is not one where you punch in at 8:00 a.m., take an hour for lunch at noon, and punch out at 5:00 p.m. In fact, the job often is most demanding, most interesting, and least flexible during those hours when many professionals have typically gone home for the evening. In a time-intensive field like student affairs, with its ambiguous borders, professionals commonly perceive the problem to be work crowding out the time that can be spent at home. Any number of tasks or opportunities at work—each with a deadline attached, can "lure [them] away form simpler pleasures that have no internal deadlines. Many professional demands are so tangible, their cost/benefit tradeoff so clear, that they seem to overrule taking the time to read to a child or trying to capture the late afternoon light" (Huff, 1996, p. 434; Weiss, 1990).

So, what should be cut? New professionals have a strong desire to make their mark at work. They view professional achievement, particularly early in a career, as the vehicle by which they will move into positions of greater authority and wider influence.

I want to move up the ladder. I like working in student life, but I cannot see doing it forever. What I really want to do is be a vice chancellor for student affairs someday. I think that I would enjoy the challenge of setting policy and working with budgets. I also think that I would be good at motivating people around me and leading them. The way to get there is to work hard now and get people to notice what I am capable of. I sometimes get frustrated, but I know that people will recognize my contributions and I will keep getting promoted. [Student Life Professional]

In addition, people typically enter student affairs because they have a passion for the work and believe that they can make a difference, as this new professional attests:

I truly enjoy my work and the gratification that I receive, especially when I advise and work with students in programming activities for the campus. [I] realize that if you make a difference in one person's/student's life it is well worth it! [Student Activities Coordinator]

Both are strong—almost intoxicating—pulls toward spending more time at work. Because their desire to build a career and be on the job more often can come into conflict with their aspiration to construct a life, student affairs administrators—particularly new professionals—can become frustrated. Their frustration can be harmful at many levels. It exacts a personal cost in stress and on relationships (Berwick, 1992; Cooper & Payne, 1988). It also may diminish effectiveness at work, as noted by this residence life professional:

When I first started this job, my life pretty much sucked. All I did was work. . . . I didn't have time for my girlfriend, my friends from undergrad, or anyone or anything else for that matter. Everything revolved around my job and I totally lost my perspective on life. Things are much better now, mostly because I figured out that I was not going to be happy unless I saved some time for myself. Also, I think that I am better at my job now because I have a lot more balance in my life. I think when I was so crazed about everything at work, I was missing a lot of things [at work].

Student affairs administrators spend much of their professional lives encouraging students to discover balance in their lives—yet they often are poor role models.

Satisfaction with one's career is important, because it leads to better feelings about one's personal life, as long as work does not become overwhelming, producing a vicious circle. When work consumes too much attention, it leaves little energy for developing satisfying personal relationships, which then encourages the investment of still more energy in work (Friedman & Greenhaus, 2000). Studying workaholics, Bonebright, Clay, and Ankenmann (2000) found that even for those individuals who were highly driven at work and enjoyed it greatly, high work involvement does not lead to increased life satisfaction or sense of purpose. They hypothesize that lack of life balance may be a factor.

Ironically, student affairs administrators spend much of their professional lives encouraging students to discover balance in their lives—to live "seamless" lives—yet they are often poor role models. They attempt to teach balance, but rarely do they practice what they preach. Particularly when they think of themselves as "on the move," their jobs tend to overtake the rest of their lives, often at the cost of a truly satisfying personal life.

I have noticed that we always teach students to live balanced lives, yet we set the worst examples. I can remember several days when I would be in the office for 12 hours, then attend a program, lead a meeting, and spend some time with students in the evening. If I was lucky, I would be in bed by 1:00 in the morning and get six hours of sleep before it was time to get up and do it all over again. [Residence Life Professional]

A new professional's enthusiasm, combined with the fast pace of the job, can further confound the boundaries of home and work. New professionals can find it difficult to segment their work and non-work lives into distinct categories and, thus, integrate the two (Nippert-Eng, 1996). It is unclear if this is intentional or if it is spillover from one to the other. Student affairs professionals work odd hours, take their work home with them, and bring their home life into the office, as these new professionals attest:

Sometimes work and home really blur. When I am at work, I am on the telephone home about something with my son, and when I am at home, I am on the phone dealing with something from work. [Student Affairs Professional]

I am new to the area and the only people that I ever socialize with are people from work. [Multicultural Affairs Professional]

Work spilling over to home seems unavoidable for many professionals. Not only is work shaping their personal life, but for many student affairs professionals, personal life is also shaping work.

INTEGRATION AND DIFFERENT VALUES

Certain types of work, like student affairs, seem to require more of an integrative view of life (Quinn, O'Neill, & Debebe, 1996). For the integrative person, professional and personal lives are almost naturally interconnected because personal values so influence both. Moreover, people find meaning in activities that are aligned with their core values. "Alignment brings meaning, and meaning brings energy. When there is no alignment, people tend to become alienated from their tasks and disengage from their work" (Quinn, O'Neill, & Debebe, 1996, p. 422).

Working toward some sort of work-life balance becomes a process of integration for many student affairs professionals, not one of defining separate arenas. In short, they are more inclined toward the seamless life than the divergent life. Moreover, because they are typically more integrative than segmented, any conceptualization of office and home, professional and personal, or work and life as separate and independent seems inconsistent with the basic values of the field.

It is hard for me to think about my life as "life" and work as "work." Most of the time, the two seem to blend together. I'm not sure this is always a good thing, but it is something I am aware of. [Residence Life Professional]

The way you divide work and life seems artificial to me. Work is such a big part of my life. Even when I am not [at work] I am thinking about it or I am with friends from work and we are telling stories or talking about things. [Student Life Professional]

Given the integration of work and life for new professionals, one useful way to frame the concept (or process) of achieving balance is through the metaphor of harmony. Walsh (1996) reflects that the professional and the personal are entwined to "create a harmony of opposites that defines us" (p. 204). Harmony is produced, however, only when both work and life are given voice simultaneously, not sequentially, just as beautiful music is the sum of several parts coming together at once. Erez (1996) offers a parallel metaphor to the notion of harmony. Career and family need not contrast but are "interrelated, like figure and background. Figures have meaning only when contrasted with the backgrounds that surround them. Similarly, the meaning of information is shaped by the context in which it appears" (p. 19).

One danger in conceptualizing work and life as a continuing quest for integration and harmony is that others, perhaps even those in supervisory and evaluative roles, may not view work and life as seamless or even as linked in any meaningful way. In fact, they may view work and family competitively, with advancement in one coming at the cost of the other.

New professionals' value of integration may conflict with their supervisors' business ethic as a "company man" who is willing to sacrifice all for the job.

I just cannot see how someone who has had a stay-at-home [spouse] for all these years can understand my situation. . . . I feel like I need to commit the same number of hours to work that the people that I work for do, but a lot of them [have] only ever needed to worry about work. [They have] never had to worry about all the household things and work at the same time, like I do. I don't even have children and it is all that I can do keep up at work without giving up spending time with my husband and doing what is important to me outside of work. [Student Affairs Professional]

The new generation of professionals is likely to feel incomplete in some way without a better balance between work and home (Vanderkolk, 1991). They are increasingly distant, intellectually, if not in fact, from the values of the "company man" who was willing to sacrifice all for the job and saw work and family in competition, with advancement in one coming at the cost of the other.

Quinn, O'Neill, and Debebe (1996) report that some professionals have a preference for actively maintaining a sharp separation between their professional and personal lives. These are not necessarily unreasonable approaches to living life and may be how some colleagues or supervisors construct their days and nights. However, given the growing number of hours work demands, and the technology that eliminates physical location as a barrier, this solution may become increasing difficult to implement. Furthermore, in a deeply involving field like student affairs, harmony seems to be a more natural approach than independence, segmentation, or separation, as is the realization that time and energy are finite resources. They are even more so without renewal, which can come from personal and family time. New professionals often perceive time and energy to be required in large measures if they are to be successful (and especially large measures if they are to be really successful). This perception, unchallenged, may lead to people ask too much of themselves.

From both research and their own sensibilities, new professionals know that they need to take the time to step back from their full work schedules, not only to avoid stress and burnout but to become better professionals. Nevertheless, they do have a strong desire to achieve in the most conventional sense of the term. They still too often view success solely or mostly in terms of measurable accomplishments on the job. Perhaps new professionals are in a "rundown". They are caught between their own "evolved" world view that values life as much as work and the standards and practices of the "company man," whose norms still govern much of what goes on at the office but which stem from an entirely different conception of work and life. In baseball, a rundown usually results in the runner being tagged out somewhere between one base and another. In life, the consequence may be similar.

UNDERSTANDING THE IMBALANCED OR OVERLY ENRICHED LIFE

The cornerstone of the search for balance prescribed in the self-help literature is identifying important values and key priorities and then using them to move toward a personal vision. This theme is also part of the scholarly literature. Values allow people to sort options and make decisions based in a personal framework. At the same time, for many new professionals, values do not fall into clear dichotomies or hierarchies (Caproni, 1997); everything seems important and nothing lends itself easily to a trade-off. Some degree of compromise is necessary, of course, but that does not make them any less unsatisfying. "The more people believe they are making a tradeoff, the less satisfied they are with their careers, their families, and their lives" (Friedman & Greenhaus, 2000, p.33). However, these compromises can be viewed in more positive ways, suggest Friedman and Greenhaus. "Tradeoffs between work and family are inevitable. The downside of these tradeoffs can be mitigated, or at least in part, by seeing them as opportunities to make conscious choices among life priorities; to become clearer about our values" (p. 38).

Nevertheless, as much as new professionals want structure in their lives through setting priorities and making tradeoffs, placing things in a hierarchy of importance is difficult—and may be beyond what most people really want to do or really know how to do. New professionals are thus left with a constant tension toward an imbalanced or overly enriched life—a life with a multitude of overlapping demands that are difficult to categorize much less reconcile.

Work and life operate within multiple dimensions at the same time, so finding balance is often like solving a four-dimensional puzzle.

I spend a lot of time working in the community through my church, which is something that I really enjoy. I also enjoy playing golf and tennis, although I used to be a lot better at both. I also just bought an old house that needs a lot of work. . . . I just started taking classes for my master's degree in higher education. I also better not forget to say that I am in a committed relationship. And I work full-time at the student life office. [Student Life Professional]

Not only do individual new professionals in student affairs play multiple roles simultaneously, but they also have varying degrees of commitment to, or engagement with, each role. "The number of roles played, the time devoted to each, the ability to play them, the amount of affect invested in each role, and the way they are played are major determinants of job satisfaction, life satisfaction, and stress" (Super, 1986, p. 99).

The unpredictable nature of student affairs makes role ambiguity and role conflict a consistent element (Ward, 1995). Stress can be a natural outcome when an individual is confronted with incompatible or unclear expectations and lacks the information to resolve the dilemma. As expected, high levels of this role stress are negatively correlated with life satisfaction (Blackhurst, Brandt, & Kalinowski, 1998). Attempting to balance the personal and the professional is, of course, an exercise that occurs within the ambiguity and conflicting ends associated with role stress.

The overly enriched and ultimately imbalanced life of the new professional may be the result of structural constraints on life balance (Kofomidos, 1997). For new professionals, these might include: pressures to focus time and energy on work; mastery-oriented performance criteria; upward career models; and demands at home and the desire to spend more time there. How student affairs professionals critique their own performance and how others evaluate their performance can also work against a healthy balance of professional aims and personal pursuits. In other words, what professionals expect of themselves and what they perceive others to expect of them do not always fit within the concept of a balanced overall life.

I hate to admit this, but I know that I have to work harder than other people to get to the same place. They all seem to pick up on things more quickly than I do. Maybe it will get better when I have some more experience, but for now I am going to do whatever it takes [to be successful]. [Student Affairs Professional]

It always seemed as though Mark set the standard for all of us. He worked until 3 in the morning and never seemed to have a life outside his job. We all knew his life was completely unhealthy and yet he seemed to get all the recognition. [Residence Life Professional]

The transition from student to entry-level professional makes balance difficult. Those coming from graduate school have been socialized to value the academic norms of collegiality and autonomy (Ward, 1995). Professional life, however, can be marked by the bureaucracy and formality more commonly associated with the business world. Student affairs graduate programs emphasize student development, which is an important part of the job of a student affairs professional, but is only one part. Another part is as an employee in the business of higher education, a worker in a competitive industry. New professionals in student affairs often feel tension between helping students, usually the primary reason they selected this career path, and fulfilling their administrative duties. Many attempt to do both, which can lead to ever-longer hours.

Simply as a structural matter, entry-level positions with high expectations of student contact make managing professional responsibilities difficult. Entry-level admissions counselors travel the most; resident directors supervise the highest number of staff members; and entry-level student activities professionals advise the most groups. Not only does this represent planned time that new professionals devote to students, but the high contact also makes them the likely first resource for the inevitable, but unpredictable, crises that require even additional time. The responsibilities typical to an entry-level position are time consuming and limit autonomy. In doing so, they heighten the potential for imbalance.

In addition, upward career aspirations exact a toll on life balance. Rarely are new professionals at the institutions or in the positions that they desire to remain in for the long run, as noted by these new professionals:

I like working at [this university], but I cannot see myself there for my whole career. It is difficult to work in student life on an urban campus and I am not sure that I want to work in student life for too much longer. I would rather be more of an administrator and possibly even teach. I would like to move back someday to a [residential campus] like where I went [as an] undergraduate. . . . I know the job market is tight and I should be thankful to have a job at all, especially because I am still working on my master's. People have told me that it is going to be hard to get a job in student affairs at a bigger school, but I guess that only makes me want to work harder. [Greek Life Advisor]

A live-in position in a residence hall is truly the entry-level in student affairs. After my second year in the residence halls, I am ready to move up. [Residence Life Professional]

Finally, these work pressures are also accompanied by demands at home and the desire to spend more time there. Claiming time for personal use even when it is much needed may be difficult, as this comment illustrates:

I try to stand up for the little bit of free time I get during the academic year. Sometimes this is met with resistance because many people assume that because I'm single, I don't have a life outside my job. [Multicultural Programming Professional]

Often new professionals will work beyond a productive pace and realize too late that they need a break. The realization may very well come during an intense time when it is impossible to take a break, exacerbating their frustration and further reducing their productivity.

I really do try to prioritize my life, but I never really get to stick to my plans because everything keeps changing so fast. I guess that makes me feel like I am not doing something right. [Setting priorities] seems to work for other people but I can't seem to get it to work for me. [Student Life Professional]

Striving for balance between work and life is such an ambitious goal that it may be an impossible one. In other words, are integration and harmony really possible? Are we seeking an idealized image that is and will always be beyond our grasp? Caproni (1997) argues that the systematic, rational planning to achieve balance that those in the work-life literature frequently champion is beyond the capability of most people. She argues that balance is an unachievable goal because of the unpredictability of life (which is certainly true in the world of student affairs) and because people are ambivalent about their goals, feelings, and choices. This may be especially the case for new professionals who are not yet aware of how to set parameters for their work. Caproni suggests that the pursuit of the balanced life inevitably results in frustration.

The inevitable frustration need not be a permanent state despite the constraints of competing priorities, multiple roles, evaluation, career aspirations, and personal interests that can overrun a new professional's life. The important point to remember is that struggles with balance and periods of imbalance are inevitable. For most people, imbalance is commonplace and balance is unusual. Balance is not easily obtained, maintained or supported, but is possible at least for periods of time.

RECOGNIZING GENDER

Pressure to find balance is significant for nearly everyone, but it can be particularly taxing for women. In a field like student affairs, where women are traditionally and increasingly well represented, any consideration of work and life must address differing personal and professional expectations grounded primarily in gender. While attitudes about men and women associated with career and home have certainly evolved, gender continues to contribute to perceptions of roles and responsibilities (Friedman & Greenhaus, 2000; Spain & Bianchi, 1996). Despite our best intentions, the dominant perceptions are that family impinges on work time for women and work encroaches on family time for men. A woman is still more likely to miss work when a child is sick, and a man is more likely to have a job that demands travel away from home. Spain and Bianchi have found that taking work home benefits the man's career, while it limits a woman's, a concept Friedman and Greenhaus term "BOP" for benefit or penalty.

Freidman and Greenhaus (2000) analyzed a number of areas within the BOP framework, reaching several conclusions about how gender affects career and family balance. Being married benefits men and is not a penalty for women. Married men reach higher positions than do unmarried men, while for women, marriage is neither help nor hindrance. Children have a positive effect on men's careers; fathers make more money and are more satisfied with their careers than are men without children. Mothers work less than their single female counterparts. They also earn less, perhaps reflecting a bias toward "face time" rather than results. Employers may be less likely to assign career-enriching work to working mothers, thus hampering career advancement for this group. Friedman and Greenhaus also identify a "satisfaction penalty" for working mothers: "[C]areer satisfaction is enhanced if we work long hours, are psychologically involved in our work, and receive opportunities for career development. Conversely, spending a lot of time on household activities detracts from our career satisfaction" (p.50).

Although both employed men and women are vulnerable to stress and have household responsibilities, women are at greater risk because they still perform the bulk of household tasks (National Research Council, 1991). United Nations data indicate that while men and women work roughly the same number of hours in a week, 56 hours and 60 hours respectively, women spend more of these hours doing unpaid work versus paid work. Women spend 24 hours each week at paid work and 32 hours at unpaid work, whereas the numbers for men are 41 hours paid and 18 hours unpaid (Spain & Bianchi, 1996). In 1990, roughly one-fifth of women were classified as homemakers, down from closer to one-third in 1980 (Spain & Bianchi, 1996). Women are more often choosing careers outside the home that accommodate family responsibilities and may more often elect to work part-time (Spain & Bianchi, 1996).

Furthermore, women working outside the home are often in positions where they have identical responsibilities and frustrations as men. Similarly, more men are electing to focus their primary attention on home and family, as well as spending more hours on housework and child care (National Research Council, 1991). As one male new professional explained:

We had our first child a couple of months ago and I have started to resent the time that I have to spend away from her working at night and sometimes on weekends. I used to not mind the hours really at all. My wife is supportive, but she gets frustrated when she is left home alone with our daughter while I am at work. [Admissions Counselor]

Although the prescribed gender roles of previous generations may be slowly eroding, there are still vast differences in the professional and personal experiences of men and women. These differences matter and deserve the consideration of both new professionals and their employers.

LESSONS TO TAKE AWAY

Balance occurs when work and life are mutually augmenting. When resources derived from one role are applied to others in fruitful ways, positive emotions initially experienced in one part of life can spill over to enrich other domains as well (Friedman & Greenhaus, 2000). Pursuing balance is a constant and dynamic effort that involves many facets: understanding the societal context; making choices; refining skills; taking time for yourself; establishing and maintaining boundaries; understanding organizational culture; working with your employer; creating roles independent of gender; remembering where you are in your career; and enjoying the journey. The complexity and multiple facets of balance are good because they mean there are many tools towards achieving it. These are the possible lessons that any professional can utilize in working toward a healthy work and personal balance.

Understanding the Societal Context

The new economy produced a societal context where jobs are less stable and opportunities are abundant. Choices as a consumer and opportunities as a worker can overwhelm people. New professionals, and student affairs educators at all levels, are not unique in their struggle for balance. There is no way that anyone can take advantage of every opportunity, career and personal, and this fact can be viewed with some comfort. Passing or missing an opportunity will likely be only temporary, because opportunities are more available in the new economy.

Making Choices

Barraged with opportunities, one must constantly decide what even to consider, let alone what to pursue. Making choices at work is difficult, but job descriptions and supervisors can help guide and prioritize. Making decisions about career and personal life are impossible without personal reflection, however. "Creating a personally fulfilling life structure is not a question of following a recipe or adhering to a set of 'tips' but rather of reflecting on the inner forces that drive one to make choices and develop a [congruent] life structure" (Kofodimos, 1997. p. 61).

The difficulty with framing the choices as a matter of life priorities is that new professionals may feel a need to change and not have time to do anything about it. They may also not even be aware that it is time to change except for some nagging feelings of discontent or burnout. Frost and Taylor (1996) recommend that people recognize that "most of the time, adjustments that we make when things are not working out are a matter of 're-tuning on the run'" (p. 491). These adjustments are critical for the time-pressed, responsibility-laden new student affairs professional. Some sort of self-reflection—knowing what one values—remains key to sorting through options and commitments and in balancing the ones accepted. Because people have such different lives, there is no single universal formula, despite what some self-help books might profess. Each new professional needs to find an approach that works. In other words, each person has to seek his or her own destiny (Walsh, 1996). It is also important to remember that any balance or satisfaction formula changes with modifications at work or in life. Updating is an essential component of reflection and planning. Choices are not final but subject to reconsideration and change (Huff, 1996).

Refining Skills

Caproni (1997) jokes that she reached an epiphany about the problems with the work-life self-help books after realizing that her newfound zest for efficiency led her to decide to wear only slip-on shoes to save time. While the quest for efficiency that is the hallmark of these books has compelling surface logic, denying societal forces and daily realities oversimplifies the balance problem. Nevertheless, self-help books have their place. Improving time management, stress management, and the professional skills they advocate give new professionals more tools to use when working towards balance.

Taking Time for Yourself

Time spent relaxing is significant to balance. Without personal time one is trading work busy-ness for personal busy-ness. This can be especially true of working women with children, who feel better about their families as they take more time for themselves (Friedman & Greenhaus, 2000). Indeed, Friedman and Greenhaus suggest that ten hours a week taken for oneself is significant in increasing overall life satisfaction.

Carving out the time can be difficult. New professionals working with their supervisors and colleagues can anticipate some of the high demand times and create buffers for personal renewal. Planning to take vacation time before or after these periods improves the professional's productivity and wellness.

Establishing and Maintaining Boundaries

Particularly with the advent of new technologies such as e-mail, the physical boundaries of old, when professionals worked at an office and then went home to pursue personal interests, barely exist anymore, if they ever did for many student affairs professionals. Yet some order must be established so new professionals feel the internal locus of control—control of their lives and responsibility for their actions—that is so important for job satisfaction (Tarver, Canada, & Lim, 1999). Boundaries need not be spatial; they can be based on issue or priority. New professionals can educate their staff and students, and perhaps their supervisor, about what personal issues are a priority for them which helps those at work to assess when an interruption at home is appropriate (Friedman, Christensen, & DeGrott, 1998). As it would be inappropriate for staff to interrupt a new professional's presentation to the board of trustees for assistance with a noise violation, educating staff about personal priorities makes it less likely they will interrupt a high personal priority with a less important work one.

Understanding Organizational Culture

Any examination of balancing the personal and the professional necessarily begins with bringing to the surface and exploring organization-level assumptions and values involving cultures and climates, behaviors and habits, and practices and procedures that either advance or hinder work-life balance. Some of the assumptions counter to a balanced life are gender roles, evaluations that stress face time rather than outcomes, and a mindset that pursuit of a satisfying personal life means a compromised career. Addressing destructive organizational cultures is easier said than done, particularly for new professionals who perceive themselves to have limited power in the organization and may be less willing to rock the boat and jeopardize their chance of moving up through the organization. In addition, learning the culture of any organization is not an overnight process. The new professional is well advised to observe and dissect information before making assumptions about the organizational culture and the norms that guide its institutional philosophy and policy (Barr, 1990; Kuh & Whitt, 1988; see also Chapters 2 and 4 in this monograph). The idea is not to attempt to change organizational culture all alone or all at once, but to think about organizational dissonance and dysfunction in terms of culture, and to act accordingly.

Working with your Employer

For any change to occur, a partnership between employers and employees is necessary. While leadership can be expected from a supervisor, the supervisor may not have the skills and certainly does not know a new professional's perspective without appropriate dialogue. New professionals can help their supervisors by initiating discussion about expectations. (See Chapter 5 in this monograph.) Professionals tend to make good decisions when employers clearly inform them of business priorities and when employers are clearly informed of the professional's personal and career priorities (Friedman, Christensen. & DeGrott, 1998). Furthermore, clear expectations are correlated with increased job satisfaction for student affairs professionals (Ward, 1995), as is autonomy and authority at work, which creates flexibility (Friedman & Greenhaus, 2000; Ward, 1995). The flexibility gives new professionals an important resource in creating balance. As new professionals seek to establish personal boundaries with their supervisors, they can model boundaries by recognizing their supervisors as whole people and respecting their supervisors' boundaries. Finally, reflection about culture and climate may prompt the new professional to consider changing jobs. "The more you learn about the fit between you and your institution, the clearer it is that you need to be somewhere [else], where you feel fewer constraints and better supported" (Gallos, 1996, p. 17).

Creating Roles Independent of Gender
It is impossible to improve the imbalance problem without addressing gender, either for men or women. At work, employers must assess career interest and provide opportunities based on an employee's ability and interest rather than making assumptions about values based on gender stereotypes (Friedman & Greenhaus, 2000). Within personal relationships, responsibilities should also be negotiated rather than denoted by gender. While gender roles are ingrained in American society, they are changing. Student affairs professionals generally are attuned to issues of equality and discrimination, and committed to their elimination; they are likely better positioned than many professionals in other fields to address gender bias.

Networking
New professionals can benefit from finding people with similar professional and/or personal situations and create social and career support by networking. Discussing balance problems helps clarify values and generates feedback for growth. Networking leads to higher job satisfaction and greater ability to balance work and family because it creates social support at work (Friedman & Greenhaus, 2000). This is more the case with women, as there is not such an effect for men. Recognizing networking by intentional community building is one way that employers can help employees to find balance.

Remembering Where You Are in Your Career
One of the dangers of relying on the advice of those who write the work-life literature is that they have already "made it." Crary (1996) writes movingly about giving up a fast-track academic career to work part-time and spend more time with her infant daughter. At the same time, she admits to spending "most of my waking hours . . . focused on my professional development in one way or another" as she ascended into her career (p. 211). Similarly, Caproni (1997) decided that balance between work and home was impossible, and she opted for the

"aesthetic perspective" of spending more time with her children and pursuing a nontraditional approach to her career. She also made these decisions from the position of someone who had already made it in her chosen field.

Not everyone in an organization has the luxury of being protected and flexible. It is much easier to choose the non-traditional path from the privileged position of senior administrator in student affairs at a resource-rich institution. New professionals likely lack the uncommitted time in their daily lives that affords the space to fully conceptualize and plan their lives and careers in the same terms as those who speak from more senior positions. Many new professionals want to move into positions with greater autonomy and broader reach. They are compelled to play the game that sometimes leads to an imbalanced life, not because they like it but because they feel they have to in order to move forward at work. Thus, the conventional wisdom that professionals must first establish their careers, then work on their personal lives, remains somewhat valid.

There is a danger in that way of thinking, however. "[Professional] rewards are uncertain, whereas we are clearly missing life if we totally give in to these pressures" (Huff, 1996). Frost and Taylor (1996) warn that a career

...can produce a portfolio of contributions and accomplishments accompanied by growth in more personal arenas. It can also reflect a life of success in one arena (e.g., the professional) and failure in another (e.g., the personal), or diminished creativity and performance in both areas. (p. 201)

Even the most career-focused and determined new professionals need to be aware of what they are potentially missing while on the career fast track. Without an awareness of the costs and benefits on both the professional and personal sides of taking a particular route, the new professional risks getting lost along the way. One new professional spoke of the need for a change in perspective this way:

It took me a while before I decided that my mental and physical health were worth more to me than being the super student affairs professional. I learned to say no and to set limits with my time. New professionals want to be super-human, but we need to know that it is okay to be human every once in a while. [Assistant Registrar]

Enjoying the Journey
We can too easily and too quickly shift our attention from what we are doing to what needs to be done next, "looking beyond" the present to anticipate what is next on the horizon. It is built into the nature of our work, perhaps. However, this can blind us to the enjoyment and the lessons to be found in what we are doing (Frost & Taylor, 1996, p. 493).

When the focus is the process or journey, not the goal or destination, spontaneity and unforeseen opportunities are central. Kofodimos (1993) distinguishes between the mountain-climbing metaphor of the traditional mastery-oriented, goal-setting approach and her favored self-awareness framework:

. . . the "mountain image" requires us to "set lofty goals and tromp arduously uphill" toward them . . . . [A more useful metaphor is the] notion of "permanent whitewater," which requires a guiding vision, an "internal locus of stability," to sustain us as we continuously negotiate the challenges of our lives. (p. 84)

Gallos' (1996) advice to new scholars applies equally to new student affairs administrators beginning their professional journey: plan well; follow your heart; enjoy the travel; replenish your spirit along the way. Planning well involves gaining some sense of the big picture, "where you are going and how you'll get there." Following your heart involves an honest assessment of what you want to do, what you do well, how you will make your contribution, and what you like to do the best. Celebrating the joys of travel is another way of saying that it is "foolish . . . to focus only on the end point and miss the scenery along the way." Finally, sustained commitment requires that you periodically replenish your spirit. "What nourishes you? What rejuvenates? The answers are different for different people. Find out what fits you" (p. 16).

Concluding Thoughts

> Without work all life goes rotten.
>
> Albert Camus
>
> Take away love and our earth is a tomb.
>
> Robert Browning
>
> The basic requirements of human existence are work and love.
>
> Sigmund Freud

Organizational theorist James P. Walsh (1996) juxtaposes these quotes to begin his short essay, "Thoughts on Integrating Work and Personal Life." A life in imbalance is necessarily incomplete. We need both work and love to prosper. A balance between the two is not available through the rote application of a formula or system, nor is it as simple as applying some time management tips. It requires that new professionals step back and truly examine their lives. It is a process that comes with potential pitfalls but also with the wonderful opportunity for thriving in both realms.

The compromises involved in the search for balance necessarily involve some frustration and disappointment. Becoming ever more efficient may be bought at the cost of some loss of attachment or flexibility, or even soul. In other words, the potential solutions to an overly enriched life might bring new and greater problems. Similarly, cutting back on work may not be fully compatible with seemingly boundless professional responsibilities or making a mark at the office. These concerns are magnified because what motivates student affairs professionals is not simply extrinsic rewards, but a true enthusiasm for what they do. Work is typically so important to student affairs professionals because it is so intertwined with personal values. They are rarely "on the clock" in a way that allows them to separate work and home easily. This passion for work and a balance of work and life are possible. The goal is to feed the passion in such a way that it fuels other aspects of one's life.

Perhaps an even greater difficulty is that anything approaching real balance between work and life is such an ambitious goal that it may be nearly impossible to attain. Balance is sought in a societal context with cultures and climates—workplace rules and procedures—that remain defined by values that conflict with a balanced life. The opportunities of the new economy, slowly changing gender roles, and the structure of positions held by new professionals are some of the forces that can cause an imbalance between work and life. Working to achieve perfect harmony between the professional and the personal is an inherently messy task that may be beyond what most people are willing to do or are capable of doing. The very difficult pursuit of an idealized image is, quite naturally, a recipe for frustration. Balance is a dynamic goal that requires constant reflection and adjustment. A realistic approach for the new professional might be to consider advice about improving skills and increasing job satisfaction, as work is particularly dominating in a new career.

However, leaving the focus at just work makes balance now or in the future a greater challenge. New professionals would do well to make what time they can for themselves, and to invest in things in their personal life that create positive overflows in their work and vice versa. Perhaps the goal is to enjoy the opportunities of enrichment and to obtain balance as often as possible. While deeply personal, the quest for balance should not be solely an individual one. It is up to everyone to address a healthy balance publicly and privately to create changes for positive people, families, organizations, and society.

REFERENCES

Ashford, S. J. (1996). The publishing process: The struggle for meaning. In P. J. Frost & M. S. Taylor (Eds.), *Rhythms of academic life: Personal accounts of careers in academia* (pp. 119-127). San Francisco: Jossey-Bass.

Barr, M. (1990). Making the transition to a professional role. In D. Coleman & J. Johnson (Eds.), *The new professional: A resource guide for student affairs professionals and their supervisors* (NASPA Monograph Series, Vol. 10). Washington, DC: National Association of Student Personnel Administrators.

Berwick, K. R. (1992). Stress among student affairs administrators: The relationship of personal characteristics and organizational variables to work related stress. *Journal of College Student Development, 33*(1), 11-19.

Blackhurst, A. E., Brandt, J. E., & Kalinowski, J. (1998) Effects of personal and work-related attributes on the organizational commitment and life satisfaction of women student affairs administrators. *NASPA Journal, 35,* 86-99.

Bonebright, C. A., Clay, D. L., & Ankenmann, R. D. (2000) The relationship of workaholism with work-life conflict, life satisfaction, and purpose in life. *Journal of Counseling Psychology, 47*(4), 469-477.

Bollier, D., & Firestone, C.M. (1997) *The networked society: How new technologies are transforming markets, organizations, and social relationships.* Aspen, CO: Aspen Institute Roundtable on Information Technology. (ERIC Document Reproduction Service No. ED417751)

Caproni, P. J. (1997). Work/life balance: You can't get there from here. *Journal of Applied Behavioral Science, 33*(1), 46-56.

Cooper, C. L., & Payne, R. (1988). *Causes, coping, and consequences of stress at work.* New York: Wiley.

Crary, M. (1996). Holding it all together. In P. J. Frost & M. S. Taylor (Eds.), *Rhythms of academic life: Personal accounts of careers in academia* (pp. 207-18). San Francisco: Jossey-Bass.

Erez, M. (1996). Rhythms of an academic's life: Crossing cultural borders. In P. J. Frost & M. S. Taylor (Eds.), *Rhythms of academic life: Personal accounts of careers in academia* (pp. 19-29). San Francisco: Jossey-Bass.

Friedman, S. D., Christensen, P. and DeGrott, J. (1998). Work and life: The end of the zero-sum game." *Harvard Business Review, 76*(6), 119-29.

Friedman, S. D. & Greenhaus, J.H. (2000). *Work and family allies or enemies? What happens when business professionals confront life choices.* New York: Oxford University Press.

Frost, P. J., & Taylor, M. S. (Eds.) (1996). *Rhythms of academic life: Personal accounts of careers in academia.* San Francisco: Jossey-Bass.

Gallos, J. V. (1996). On becoming a scholar: One woman's journey. In P. J. Frost & M. S. Taylor (Eds.), *Rhythms of academic life: Personal accounts of careers in academia* (pp. 11-18). San Francisco: Jossey-Bass.

Huff, A. S. (1996). Professional and personal life. In P. J. Frost & M. S. Taylor (Eds.), *Rhythms of academic life: Personal accounts of careers in academia* (pp. 429-434). San Francisco: Jossey-Bass.

International Labour Organization (2001). Key Indicators of the Labour Market 2001-2002. Geneva: International Labour Office.

Jackson, S. E. (1996). Dealing with the overenriched life. In P. J. Frost & M. S. Taylor (Eds.), *Rhythms of academic life: Personal accounts of careers in academia* (pp. 351-355). San Francisco: Jossey-Bass.

Kofodimos, J. (1993). *Balancing act: How managers can integrate successful careers and fulfilling personal lives.* San Francisco: Jossey-Bass.

Kofodimos, J. (1997). Interpreting lessons learned: A comment on Paula Caproni's journey into balance. (*Journal of Applied Behavioral Science, 33* 1), 57-63.

Kuh, G. D., & Whitt, E. J. (1988). *The invisible tapestry: Culture in American colleges and universities* (ASHE-ERIC Higher Education Reports, No. 1). Washington, DC: Association for the Study of Higher Education.

National Research Council (1991). *Work and family: Policies for a changing workforce.* Washington, DC: National Academy Press.

Nippert-Eng, C. E. (1996). *Home and work: Negotiating boundaries though everyday life.* Chicago: University of Chicago Press.

Quinn, R. E., O'Neill, R. E., & Debebe, G. (1996). Confronting the tensions in an academic career. In P. J. Frost & M. S. Taylor (Eds.), *Rhythms of academic life: Personal accounts of careers in academia* (pp. 421-427). San Francisco: Jossey-Bass.

Reich, R. B. (2002). *The future of success.* New York: Vintage Books

Spain D., & Bianchi, S. M. (1996). *Balancing act: Motherhood, marriage and employment among American women.* New York: Russell Sage Foundation.

Super, D. (1986). Life career roles: Self-realization in work and leisure. In D. Hall (Ed.), *Career development in organizations* (pp. 95-119). San Francisco: Jossey-Bass.

Tarver, D., Canada, R., & Lim, M. (1999). The relationship between job satisfaction and locus of control among college student affairs administrators and academic administrators. *NASPA Journal, 36*(2), 96-105.

Vanderkolk, B. S. (1991). *The work and family revolution: How companies can keep employees happy and business profitable.* New York: Facts on File.

Walsh, J. P. (1996). Thoughts on integrating work and personal life (and the limits of advice). In P. J. Frost & M. S. Taylor (Eds.), *Rhythms of academic life: Personal accounts of careers in academia* (pp. 203-206). San Francisco: Jossey-Bass.

Ward, Lee. (1995). Role stress and propensity to leave among new student affairs professionals. *NASPA Journal, 33*(1), 35-44.

Weiss, R. S. (1990). *Staying the course: The emotional and social lives of men who do well at work.* New York: Free Press.

CHAPTER 8

Pathways to Success in Student Affairs

FLORENCE A. HAMRICK AND BRIAN O. HEMPHILL[1]

ongratulations! The strains of "Pomp and Circumstance" and "Alma Mater" are fading. Final assistantship and practicum duties have been wrapped up, and papers and exams are no more. Fond hugs and good-byes have been exchanged with classmates at spring picnics. The long-anticipated full-time job in student affairs is in sight or even an actuality. Perhaps you already have a year or two of full-time student affairs work experience behind you. Your diploma is in hand, but if you are lucky, learning will not cease.

In many ways, a first full-time position in student affairs is an embarkation, the beginning of one's professional career. Early career experiences provide a base for starting or continuing the processes of determining what career advancement will mean, for working toward actualizing these goals, and for evaluating choices and goals in light of new information and emerging trends. Career advancement considerations include mulling over options for future professional positions, thinking about various types of institutional work settings, and deciding whether (or when) to pursue graduate work—most often a doctoral degree. While these are separate decisions, they also represent learning processes espoused by John Dewey (1926) that entail collecting information and, more important, reflecting on individual experiences. This process of reflection brings personal meaning to the new information and assists with identifying options. This chapter provides information to help new professionals as they envision their own careers in student affairs. After discussing career path development and professional maturation, we discuss strategic considerations in career advancement.

[1] The authors wish to thank the following individuals who generously shared their expertise and quotes for use in this chapter: Karl Brooks, Joan Claar, Patrick Day, Kristi Gimmel Becker, Dennis Golder, Sandra Gonzalez-Torres, Eric Hartman, James Holmen, Joi Lewis, Michelle Moore, Augustine Pounds, Dan Robinson, Mary Beth Snyder, and Mary Spellman. We also wish to thank the new 14 new professionals who attended our focus group session at the Fall 1996 Iowa State Personnel Association annual conference and contributed their insights regarding career advancement issues and concerns.

DETERMINING CAREER PATHS

Career fields and, at times, large organizations specify career paths or ladders for new employees that will maximize the possibility that they will eventually enter senior level management jobs. Higher education career paths are much less well defined, since there are multiple paths that can lead to the top of the opportunity pyramid (Moore, 1984; Task Force, 1990; Twombly, 1990). While the idea of a career path remains a viable guiding notion for new professionals because of the planning and focus it encourages, your career path will most likely be an individual creation influenced by mentors, supervisors, colleagues, and others. Looking ahead, looking around, and looking over your shoulder may provide the best analytic perspective from which to identify personally viable paths, including previously unseen spurs and switchbacks. Trends in student affairs and higher education such as "right-sizing" challenge the wisdom of relying on prefabricated career paths to direct individual choice, since current assumptions about institutional needs and goals may not hold in the future. The goal instead should be to make the best possible career decisions with the best information available. The following sections on personal, environmental, and institutional factors provide perspectives for new professionals as they make plans for their careers in student affairs and higher education.

Personal Factors

Understanding your motivations for engaging in a particular type of work will help you define the work settings that can provide you with the rewards you seek. Derr (1986) proposed a typology of five career orientations such as "getting ahead" and "getting balanced" (pp. x-xi) to help individuals and organizations match motivations with desired rewards. Individuals most concerned with getting ahead are predominantly motivated and rewarded by promotions and money; those concerned with balance are more motivated and rewarded by flexible work environments and measures of deference to family responsibilities and personal pursuits. Depending on the person's life-stage, motivations and preferred rewards may also shift. For example, one college president who was formerly a student affairs administrator put a premium on balance during his early career: "[Working as a senior administrator] would have distracted so much from family life when our youngsters were in their formative years. We would have paid a price for absenteeism that I don't think I would have recovered from as a dad and as a husband." The process of lifelong development begins in childhood, and as that process moves forward our evolving commitments and priorities are often reflected in work and career choices.

Dual career marriages and partnerships, divorce or termination of an intimate relationship, successful cultivation of support networks, birth and growth of children, blended family concerns, and needs of aging parents are familiar examples of personal considerations that impact career decisions, especially with regard to position or geographic mobility. Despite popular conceptions that women professionals generally are less mobile than men because of personal and family considerations, Sagaria and Johnsrud's research (1988) on position change patterns demonstrated that gender gaps in geographic mobility and rates of position changes were not significantly wide. Additionally, Nobbe and Manning (1997) concluded that women student affairs administrators who were also mothers enjoyed motherhood as a counterbalance to work-related stress.

Environmental Factors

Many environmental forces have implications for professionals working in higher education who seek job change and advancement to senior administrative positions. For example, recent years of stable or declining state and federal support for higher education have been accompanied by a less seasonal and more tentative student affairs job market in which anticipated and funding-contingent positions are advertised along with actual vacancies (Janasiewicz & Wright, 1993). As in most professions, the field of student affairs offers a kind of "opportunity pyramid," with many entry-level positions and comparatively few senior-level positions. Consequently, only a small proportion of today's new professionals will attain senior administrative positions. Additionally, Evans (1988) explained that supervisory configurations in higher education have relatively few levels and result in career ladders with fewer vertical rungs and wider career "steps," suggesting that dramatic vertical movement occurs less frequently than horizontal job change. Finally, since senior administrators also move horizontally among deanships or vice-presidencies at more than one campus, not all senior administrative positions are filled from the available pipeline of mid-level student affairs administrators. One outgrowth of this is the growing research on mid-level managers in student affairs, much of which identifies positions at this level as more than simply preparation for senior administrative positions, thus prompting a re-examination of traditional assumptions of career success and achievement (Belch & Strange, 1995; Fey & Carpenter, 1996; Gordon, Strode, & Mann, 1993).

At least one additional factor plays a role in the high level of competition for senior student affairs positions: Successful candidates for these positions also come from the ranks of faculty and other administrative specialties and do not always have direct experience or educational preparation in student affairs administration or higher education (Task Force, 1990). Such hiring decisions are most often made by presidents and, although senior student affairs administrators who hold doctoral degrees in higher education regard the doctorate as useful preparation, presidents and senior academic affairs officers (except for community colleges) generally regard the higher education doctorate as useful but not essential for a senior student affairs officer (Townsend & Wiese, 1992). We will return to the issue of doctoral study later in this chapter.

Institutional Factors

Institutional factors also influence career path development, since individuals work on specific campuses as well as in the broader field of student affairs. Specific decisions regarding positions and responsibilities, restructuring, and professional development are made at the individual institutional, division, or program level. Institutions or divisions may offer formalized internship and cross-training opportunities (e.g., Robinson & Delbridge-Parker, 1991), but new professionals may also discover barriers to their professional development such as cost of program attendance and lack of information about these opportunities (Young, 1994). Division and program support for professional advancement of staff vary widely, and job candidates must not be hesitant to inquire about the levels and types of support available to staff members. However, in one study of institutional financial constraints and implications for student services programs, enhancing staff knowledge and providing staff training ranked relatively low (6th and 11th, respectively) on the list of 13 productivity strategies provided (Rames, 2000). These results suggest that investments in staff development are not necessarily regarded as important investments in productivity. Especially during times of economic shortfalls, availability of funded professional development opportunities for staff members can be limited.

Although prolonged job-hopping can eventually raise suspicion, new professionals need not worry that a first negative job experience will be fatal to their careers.

New professionals may begin a first job only to be surprised by an unforeseen mismatch between themselves and their positions or an uneasy institutional fit overall (e.g., Shriberg & Wester, 1994). Not everyone finds a first professional position that "clicks," and job turnover in entry-level positions is often high. One new professional remarked: "There's been a high turnover lately among the six program coordinator positions, so even in my second year I am the second most senior program coordinator." Regular turnover at entry-level positions thus also plays a facilitative role as new professionals change jobs possibly one or two more times in an effort to find appropriate challenges and environmental supports. Although prolonged job-hopping can eventually raise suspicion, new professionals need not worry that a first negative job experience will be fatal to their careers. The first author of this chapter spent one long and relatively unsettling year in her first professional position before locating a position that provided a much closer match for her skills and work style.

Some student affairs positions may not be located within a division or department of student affairs, especially as many campuses take a decentralized approach to student services delivery. These jobs can offer different perspectives and attractive work settings. According to one professional currently serving as admissions and financial aid officer in an MBA program office:

The School of Business here is very much like a small college, but with the additional benefits of being in a university community. Personally, my primary efforts are spent on recruitment and admissions, but I sit in meetings to discuss the curriculum, students' preparation and progress through the program, placement issues, and evaluation of our program's fit with employers' needs. I know what's going on throughout the school. In other admissions positions, I would bring in students and then never see them again, but here I work with them throughout their two years here and afterwards. I have a much greater understanding of the student experience from beginning to end.

For personal reasons (e.g., priorities, aspirations), and for environmental and institutional reasons (e.g., job market dynamics, professional development resources, short vertical career ladder), a career path is more likely to result from an individual's best judgment rather than from a pre-specified route to some culminating position. Some of the aforementioned environmental and institutional factors, however, are also cited as sources of frustration and reasons for leaving the student affairs field.

PATHS, DIGRESSIONS, AND ASPIRATIONS

One early study placed the attrition rate from student affairs jobs, 1 to 10 years after degree completion, at 39% among master's and doctoral recipients (Burns, 1982). A subsequent study of a 10-year span of master's graduates from one graduate program determined a lower overall attrition rate of 33% (Holmes, Verrier, & Chisholm, 1983). Although 80.9% were employed in student affairs jobs one year after graduation, only 39% of respondents held student affairs positions five years later. The combined rate for graduates employed in student affairs or other higher education positions was 89.3% after one year and 58.5% after six years (Holmes et al., 1983).

It is not clear whether these attrition proportions are indicative of potential problems characteristic of student affairs work or perhaps instead reflect demographics of an increasingly mobile and career-changing society (Lorden, 1998). In 1990, the student affairs field was characterized as being less competitive financially than other careers available to master's degree recipients (Task Force, 1990). Documented factors related to attrition in student affairs include: limited opportunities to grow professionally, pursue scholarship, or use knowledge; limited mobility due to relocation difficulties, hiring practices, or limited or unclear career paths (Evans, 1988); age (attrition increases with age); years past the master's degree (Burns, 1982); and role conflict, stress, and ambiguity (Ward, 1995). On the other hand, advantages of working in student affairs include: the quality of life within an academic community, professional association involvement, research and development opportunities, and intrinsically rewarding work (Task Force, 1990). According to one study, satisfaction with career choice averaged higher than 80% among new professionals (Holmes et al., 1983). New professionals should carefully consider sets of perceived advantages and disadvantages as they plan their careers.

Furthermore, more is now known about the estimated gender and broad ethnic categorizations of the pool of new student affairs professionals, including 67-68% women and 12-15% African American, (Turrentine & Conley, 2001). However, it is less clear how individuals within these and other demographic categories proportionately or disproportionately experience attrition from the profession.

As part of a meaningful life, we pursue careers that are meaningful. Career advancement can be construed as a series of positions that serve as stepping stones to a desired culminating position; career advancement can also be regarded as a process directed toward greater actualization of one's potential as a student affairs educator (Manning, 1994). To prompt personal deliberations on values, self, and actualization, Rhatigan (1996) offers the following:

What directs your life? What are the sources of the answers you have achieved? How does this bear on your work? Often the word "journey" is used, an appropriate metaphor, reminding us that the answers to these questions are not always the same, even in an individual life. Most importantly, the word "journey" recognizes movement toward a destination. The pursuit occurs across time in our relationships with people and in our journey into the self. (p. 73)

Although many student affairs professionals design their career paths leading to upper administrative positions, not all aspirants will realize that goal and some professionals do not even aspire to it. Although career ambitions often are vertically directed or vertically realized, they need not be that alone. Common to most concepts of career advancement is an ideal of maturity that can be achieved in part through professional experiences.

MATURING AS A PROFESSIONAL

A college president who was formerly a student affairs administrator remarked: "Were I to have been offered a senior level administrative position before I had reached a certain experiential level and maturity in my own career, I would not have been able to do this job. Impossible. Absolutely impossible." To call an individual a seasoned professional is to recognize his or her professional maturity, capabilities, and readiness for more complex challenges. As a result of work experience, new professionals develop maturity in their own practice. Although maturity is not directly associated with mere accumulation of experience, a person's skills, capabilities, and instincts can, nevertheless, be refined and developed with the practice that comes through experience.

As a new professional, it is often difficult to remember Scher and Barr's (1979) admonition that "individuals must carefully attend to their survival as people who have professional jobs rather than as professionals who also have a personal life" (p. 530). Student affairs work is frequently characterized by long days and evenings involved in meetings, working with students and staff members, planning, and learning. It is not surprising to learn that being new to the profession was a significant factor in predicting job-related stress in student affairs (Berwick, 1992). New professionals are getting acclimated to the culture of a new college or university and searching for a personal fit with its staff, campus, and local community all at the same time. This acclimation may be particularly critical for people of color and gay, lesbian, bisexual, and transgendered professionals as they seek communities or networks offering support and acceptance. In the case of new professionals who continue to work at the same institution from which they earned their degree, they must make transitions in practice and perspective from student or paraprofessional to full-time professional staff member. This effort can be further complicated by the perceptions of colleagues, support staff, and others who still view them as students. Supervisors often anticipate such concerns and work directly with new professionals (and staff members) to ease this transition.

When asked about their transitions from being the new person at their campuses to being a contributor and leader, new professionals often spoke in terms of finding their footing and finding their voice. Consider the three excerpts that follow:

I had the opportunity to work for two directors in two different career services offices as a coordinator prior to this position. As a coordinator I tended to rely on advice from the directors and learn from them. Much of what I learned was constructive and useful to my understanding of how I would organize and administer my own career services program, and some of what I learned helped me decide what I would not want to do and how I would not want to be. Now that I am a director, I feel very confident about my career services knowledge and my professional abilities. In addition, I do not hesitate to make major decisions on my own, and I am responsible for my department's budget. I have also challenged myself by assuming leadership roles in two state professional associations. Through this involvement I have been able to provide advice and mentoring to current graduate students and new professionals. [Career Services Director]

In my experience, I felt less like a newcomer when problems arose and my staff and supervisors began to look to me for solutions and suggestions instead of thinking, "Well, he's new here." Then I started to be heard and acknowledged as a resource and as someone with expertise who can help us get from point A to point B. It has been important for me to listen and learn about the campus's history and culture and then show that I have a true understanding of the issue or problem at hand. For me, colleagues' feedback was the signal that I was less "new" and on target with my understandings of the campus and important issues here. I brought my own personal philosophies of working with students and groups, and my own sets of theoretical approaches, but I try to match these with what I continue to learn about the campus. It will be important for me to complete an academic year, too, so that I experience a full cycle on campus. [Student Activities Director]

I remember coming [here] and being almost overwhelmed with all there was to learn about the field, my job, the college, and my new home, and I wondered when, if ever, I would feel that sense of not being new anymore. I had this conversation with friends from grad school who were going through similar things. It was a gradual process for me of getting to know people and feeling comfortable in a new place. I began feeling that sense of not being the "new professional" sometime during the spring and summer of my first year. I think it takes a solid year to begin to understand the cycle and rhythms of an institution. I knew I was emerging as a not so new professional when I began taking on tasks because they made sense and needed to be done. And when people began calling me to serve on committees and work on projects because they knew my skills and interest areas, not because the project fit my job description. So I guess the realization was gradual for me but it was triggered when I noticed more and more requests for my participation or new projects coming into my area. What helped me most in making this transition was confidence in my skills and preparation and in immersing myself in the job and the institutional culture. [Study Abroad Coordinator]

Much of finding your footing is getting used to a new campus and new ways of doing things, and finding your voice is realizing that you, as a new staff member, have valuable insights and perspectives to share. According to Van Maanen (1983), professional socialization is a reciprocal and ongoing process. As the new professionals above make clear, we should not underestimate the necessity of learning the culture and traditions of the campus since new professionals' contributions are often judged in light of their grasp of institutional nuances. By considering their own perspectives in light of their growing knowledge of the campus, new professionals can reach mature judgments about the degree to which their ideas will be welcomed or resisted.

This learning process can also deepen knowledge about oneself and one's own strengths and weaknesses, presenting opportunities for reflection-in-action (Schon, 1983) and the increased development of reflective practice. The practices are not so much a product of formal coursework and formal learning, but they are enhanced through internships and practica, watching, participating in mentoring relationships, and personal trial and error (Brown, Podolske, Kohles, & Sonnenberg, 1992; Richmond & Sherman, 1991). The learning involved in these opportunities underscores the critical importance of a solid institutional fit with an environment that supports and encourages risk-taking as a form of learning and professional development.

New professionals may not have decided on specific job targets or strategies for attaining them, but entry-level professional positions provide opportunities to observe, learn from, and work with established practitioners who may serve as models if not mentors. There can be rich opportunities for reflective learning, cultivating professional instincts, and "catching" an assortment of skills that are not often the subject of formal educational settings (Task Force, 1990). Examples of these competencies include developing a feel for optimal decision timing, dealing with consequences of decisions, and delegating expediently and appropriately (Appleton, Briggs, & Rhatigan, 1978). More recently, a meta-analysis of prior studies identified skills such as administration, management, and research/evaluation/assessment as well as knowledge bases and personal qualities that together comprised the skills of a successful student affairs administrator (Lovell & Kosten, 2000). A study of skills desirable among student affairs mid-level managers revealed similar results concerning personal management, but included a higher ranking for student contact and a somewhat lower ranking for research and evaluation skills (Saunders & Cooper, 1999).

Mature practice is critical for student affairs practitioners who are called on to deal with some of the most puzzling and distressing issues on campuses. Student affairs professionals bring their maturity and professional capabilities to bear on developments in higher education such as the current challenges and opportunities posed by technology, campus diversity, and increased student activism. Although we try to anticipate the topics of future challenges, we do not have a crystal ball. Preparation for meeting challenges includes readying ourselves to maintain a positive disposition to changes and challenges through reflective and mature practice. Change can rack a campus, yet change also provides opportunities for the transformation of our campuses, practices, and attitudes (Rhoads & Black, 1995).

STRATEGIC ISSUES IN CAREER ADVANCEMENT

Identifying and addressing strategic career advancement issues are major challenges and concerns for most new professionals. Mentoring and professional association involvement are also integral factors in career advancement, and these issues are addressed in detail elsewhere in this monograph. The following sections address the critical yet often puzzling issues of doctoral degree attainment, conventional and non-conventional career paths, institutional crossovers, and accrual mobility in student affairs.

Practical Experience and the Doctorate
According to one student affairs professional:

Young professionals in student affairs should be striving to achieve educational excellence. While a doctorate degree might not be the be-all and end-

all for every aspiring new professional, it should be strongly considered. For student affairs professionals in the field to gain credibility from colleagues (and the all-influential faculty), they must contribute to the academic experience of students, document those contributions and their effects, and relay them to the entire campus community, including students, faculty, and administrative colleagues. Simply put, pursuing a doctorate degree is a commitment beyond practice. It signifies the pursuit of knowledge that contributes to a field promoting personal growth and development. Young professionals who have an understanding of the complexities of higher education should see the doctorate degree as an opportunity to continue discovering themselves as learners, while promoting both professional and intellectual skill building.

Does advancement in student affairs require a doctoral degree? This question is frequently asked by new professionals yet is difficult to answer because of the many related contingencies such as position aspirations and types of institutions. Those who aspire to professional positions as directors (e.g., of student activities, of multicultural affairs) may be able to attain their goal with a master's degree, but this depends on the traditions, expectations, size, and organizational structure of the college or university. According to Rickard (1985):

Position listings in *The Chronicle of Higher Education* capsulize, both implicitly and explicitly, institutional values and expectations. Position requirements typically include degree minimums, years of experience, and experience in similar kinds of institutions. In a study of 103 vacancy listings for senior and mid-level student affairs officers, four-year public institutions expressed a clear preference for a doctorate, while private institutions required a master's degree. The top-ranked requirement for both public and private was experience in similar kinds of institutions. (p. 5)

Increasing numbers of job advertisements in *The Chronicle of Higher Education* contain the phrase, "master's required; doctorate preferred," but there are no clear patterns of expectations among colleges and universities because of institutional differences in philosophy, image, and other factors. In discussing the importance of the doctoral degree as a professional credential, one vice president and dean of students remarked:

You do not have to have a doctorate to be a dean of students or a vice president for student affairs, as a select few institutions do not require one. However, by having an earned doctorate, your opportunities to be selected as a finalist from a candidate pool will increase significantly.

While position announcements sometimes list a doctoral degree as a preferred (not required) qualification, the doctorate broadens the range of institutions at which a candidate may successfully compete for a dean or vice president position.

According to a study of senior student affairs administrators, work experience emerged as the primary qualifier for advancement and was ranked as more important than one's terminal degree field of study (Lunsford, 1984). A subsequent study of college and university officials (i.e., presidents, vice presidents for academic affairs) involved in selecting senior student affairs administrators indicated that the experience gained through earning a doctoral degree helps senior student affairs administrators be competitive in job searches (Komives, 1993).

Many higher education and student affairs doctoral programs require that applicants have several years of full-time work experience—usually, at minimum, between two and five—as a criterion for admission. Although opinions range widely about the need for full-time experience, obtaining a doctorate without prior full-time experience can be detrimental to the student. Work experience provides a valuable basis for practical reflection as part of doctoral study. Further, new doctoral recipients may find themselves regarded as overqualified for some positions by virtue of education yet underqualified for others by virtue of experience, negatively affecting their marketability. A professional who has earned a master's degree and worked with program development, supervision, policies, procedures, and budgets is more attractive than an applicant with a doctorate and little or no prior experience in these areas.

A student affairs professional who served as a dean of students and a vice president for student services echoed this view:

The professional standards and guidelines for student services programs support the popular belief that student services leaders must have substantial work experiences in one of the functional areas of student services and an advanced degree to command respect for their leadership on campus. Part of commanding respect comes from a working knowledge and experience in student personnel.

The increasing selectivity of the job market and the adherence to more formalized hiring practices also suggest that competitive candidates will demonstrate a balance of professional study and experience (Birch, 1984). Again, no one road map guides new professionals to success, but new professionals who gain theoretical knowledge and practical experience in program development, supervision, policy development, and budgeting will open doors to advancement in student affairs.

Conventional vs. Non-Conventional Career Paths
New professionals in student affairs are confronted immediately with career decisions that may appear confusing, a situation complicated by different individuals giving different advice on career strategies. This section provides an overview of the traditional and non-traditional career paths that are representative of current professionals in student affairs.

Historically, those who aspired to be senior student affairs administrators started their careers in residence life (Birch, 1984). Perhaps this is not surprising when compared to Richmond and Benton's (1988) study of placement results in which the largest category of new professionals in student affairs (i.e., regardless of career aspiration) found their first professional position in residence life, despite initially lower anticipations of a residence life job. This career beginning was also common during the 1960s and 1970s when residence life was viewed as a key starting point because of the variety of experiences a new professional acquired in the residence hall setting. In residence life, new professionals observe and influence student development by managing responsibilities from student counseling to judicial affairs, experiences commonly seen as the cornerstone of a successful student affairs career. The experiences of one new master's degree recipient suggest that a residence life position also provides a departure point for closer involvement with, and understanding of, other programs in student affairs:

Student affairs as a profession is similar to other professions . . . there are those who believe only one path should be traveled in an effort to be successful. However, I come from the school of thought that there are many directions one can take to be successful in our field. Although I have taken what historically has been thought of as a traditional path through residence life, I think it imperative to be familiar and involved with other areas of student affairs as well as other facets of the university . . . I think the contemplation should not be if one will be limited because of the choice to pursue residence life, admissions, multicultural affairs, or student activities. The contemplation should be more about you as a new professional limiting yourself. Any facet of student affairs will most likely provide an avenue to pursue your ultimate goals. One must be careful not to build walls and close oneself in nor allow others to apply such limitations.

Today, new professionals take multiple routes to the deanship. In the 1980s and 1990s, an increasing number of practitioners began their careers in student activities, academic advising, financial aid, volunteer services, career services, multicultural affairs, and admissions, leading to increased diversity in background experiences (J. Claar, personal communication, January 2002; M. B. Snyder, personal communication, January 2002). One advantage of this variety of entry points to student affairs is that new professionals with primary interests in areas other than residence life can be accommodated earlier in their careers. It is unclear to what extent beliefs persist about residence life as a preferred basis for a student affairs career. Time will tell whether increasing numbers of professionals with non-traditional career beginnings are able to realize their career advancement goals. As the above individual suggested, new professionals gain a tremendous advantage in the job search by acquiring early expe-

130

rience in multiple areas of student affairs (e.g., residence life, student activities, career services, multicultural affairs) through full-time work and also through internships and practica.

In some cases, new professionals may fear that several successive years in one functional area will typecast them as an expert in one area and limit their marketability for generalist administrative positions. Sustained expertise in one area provides a valuable track record of success and an additional set of opportunities for advancement within that specialty, but professionals concerned about being locked into one area can seek out committee assignments and collaborative projects in other student affairs areas or within professional associations in order to demonstrate a breadth of commitments and expertise. For new professionals, positions that entail responsibilities in more than one student affairs area may be particularly attractive. One example of such a position, often referred to as a "split" or "joint" appointment, is a job that specifies 60% time in a residence life appointment and 40% time in career services. Although this arrangement can offer valuable skill-building opportunities, new professionals and their supervisors must take care to ensure that the "split" does not become two full-time jobs that one person is expected to perform.

Building transferable skills does not guarantee that a move to the desired specialty area will follow. Such transfers can be more or less difficult to accomplish depending on, for example, the existing number of professionals with the requisite knowledge base and experience. Participating in cross-training experiences, pursuing continuing education, and holding split positions can help professionals demonstrate a new set of goals and skills to a prospective employer.

Determining a career path is not an easy task, but new professionals can take advantage of a valuable source of information by participating in professional conferences. As student affairs professionals, we advise students that one critical key to success in college is involvement; the same advice applies to our own careers. The networking that occurs at conferences enhances skills and provides insight into various career opportunities. By participating in conferences and other professional development programs, newcomers can learn, sharpen abilities, and evaluate career decisions while they increase their marketability by gaining "the experience and skills of a knowledgeable professional that can translate into preferential standing for job placement" (Allen, 1987, p. 11).

Institutional Crossovers: Public and Private

Working in three private and two public institutions, my career choice was one of professional development. Except for my residential life experiences, I had become a generalist. Although I realized many employers, especially those in small private liberal arts institutions, seek generalists, it was important for me to find a job that would help me develop my skills in one

131

particular area of student development. [Admissions Professional]

New professionals obtain employment in any number of different types of institutions—doctoral-granting universities, comprehensive institutions, liberal arts colleges, community colleges, and vocational technical colleges. Of the types mentioned, community colleges represent the fastest growing sector of higher education (O'Banion, 1997). As the proportion of student affairs career opportunities in community colleges continues to increase, so will the knowledge base about strategic career issues characteristics of student affairs professionals in community colleges. Due to the current paucity of information on these issues as they relate to community college, this section focuses on two types of institutions commonly discussed with respect to professional crossover decisions: doctoral granting universities (i.e., large and public) and liberal arts colleges (i.e., small and private).

Professionals in the field of student affairs may wonder whether they can or should "cross over" to different types of institutions in the course of their careers and question how competitively crossover candidates are regarded. The admissions professional quoted above observed that one of the major differences between public and private institutions is being a generalist or a specialist. New professionals in public colleges and universities are traditionally hired to perform one or two major duties and are not expected, and perhaps not encouraged, to venture into other areas of responsibility. Most public institutions have a large student affairs staff; therefore, individuals specialize in specific programmatic areas and may need to do so for professional advancement. Middle- and upper-level managers in large public institutions have more opportunities to venture into other areas of student services as they supervise diverse program offices or plan cooperative ventures.

Student affairs positions at small, private colleges and universities are more fluid in nature, and professionals (including new professionals) are expected to move beyond expertise in any one narrow specialty. Many private colleges expect their multicultural affairs and student activities staffs to play active roles in residence life, health services, volunteer services, and freshman orientation. In short, private colleges tend to expect new professionals to be generalists. A new professional must possess the skills and confidence as well as the desire to work outside of his or her area of expertise.

Some employers are impressed by professionals who have worked in a variety of settings early in their careers; those who work in one setting for seven to 10 years may find themselves defined by their prior choice of institutional type. Kaufmann (1983) also found that faculty members on selection committees were wary of candidates attempting such crossovers. For example, an administrator in a small, private institution may have difficulty moving to a large public college or university or from a two-year to a four-year institution. Although there are no set rules in this area, institutional crossovers can be accomplished early in a new professional's career as a means of determining whether a public or private environment best matches his or her professional needs and goals, personality, or preferred work style. Once professionals are established and identified in a given area, they may find it difficult to change the perceptions of others who associate them with a particular type of institution. Direct experience is one of the best determinants of fit with respect to institutional type. As is true for students, we grow and develop best when we are in a comfortable yet stimulating environment that includes but transcends working relationships:

The notion of having the opportunity to work with, and for, good professionals contributes to the "goodness-of-fit" principle. But there is more to the principle than good working relationships. One needs to feel equally good about the quality of the new environment. (Birch, 1984, p. 47)

One faculty member and student affairs administrator recommends that new professionals experience both settings during the course of their academic preparation:

New professionals in graduate school must be sensitive to the issue of marketability during the process of completing an academic program. Practicums and internships are excellent ways to take a close look at the market availability for new professionals. It is critical that they develop courses of study which provide the opportunity to experience both public and private institutions.

On the advice of a Dean of Students, new professionals should subsequently evaluate and re-evaluate their decisions:

New professionals must realize that the decision to work in a public or private institution does not have to be permanent. Select the best setting for yourself but realize the career decision-making process does not end with your first job. Research and evaluate the different settings and make a professional decision about your future.

New professionals must ask themselves several questions regarding an institution's traditions, environment, and values, and consider how the answers correlate with their own personality, values and beliefs. Wise decisions will contribute to a rewarding student affairs career.

Promotions and Accrual Mobility in Student Affairs

In student affairs administration, the prevailing attitude seems to be that the way to move up is to move out—to move on to another institution or position (Lunsford, 1984). Further, according to Burkhalter (1984), an administrator in student affairs will generally work for five different institutions during his or her career. Accrual mobility and internal promotions, however, may account for an increasing number of promotional opportunities. Accrual mobility "occurs through evolved jobs in which the employee accrues responsibility and/or knowledge well beyond normal growth in the job" (Miner & Estler, 1985, p. 121) and results in the creation of a new position or unit in recognition of the employee's growth that matches an institutional need. Consider the following assistant dean of students' career thus far:

While initially content to do the proverbial "two year tenure" of most new professionals, I found that the opportunity for accumulated knowledge and experience was increasing exponentially each year I remained with the university. After year three, I was regularly engaged in institutional activity far beyond any that could have been experienced in that time period by taking a position at another college or university. In addition, I found myself with a promotion and an opportunity to attend graduate school at minimal cost. Despite the rural isolation, the scarcity of African American professionals, and the newness of my functional area, extending my stay was one of the most professionally profitable decisions I ever made.

Increasingly competitive job markets may well establish an atmosphere in which professionals can view their careers... as long-term commitments to a particular higher education institution.

Financial constraints often cause institutional administrators to re-evaluate potential job openings. During times of severe financial stress, colleges and universities may reduce the number of job opportunities for both new and seasoned professionals (e.g., Burkhalter, 1984). Additionally, new organizational structures have emerged with student affairs offices reporting to academic affairs administrators or residence life programs reporting to business officers. And finally, because of financial constraints, the duties of a departing staff member are often distributed temporarily or permanently among the remaining staff.

Decreases in institutional financial resources have prompted many changes that will impact careers in student affairs and may result in longer "insider" affiliations with one institution (Sagaria & Dickens, 1990) and a subsequent intra-institutional career path. A career at one institution may also proceed through the process of accrual mobility. The professional quoted above had a successful career start as an insider, since he began as the university's coordinator of multicultural services and was promoted to assistant dean of students two years later. In student affairs, advancement through accrual mobility or by an inside path provides an alternative to a more typical assumption that position advancements always occur inter-institutionally. Increasingly competitive job markets may well establish an atmosphere in which professionals can view their careers, or significant portions of them, as long-term commitments to a particular higher education institution.

CONCLUSIONS AND RECOMMENDATIONS

Career advancement is an ongoing process. As careers evolve, individuals, institutions, and social and market trends also evolve, so new professionals are well-advised to remain aware of personal and environmental developments and the implications for their intended career paths. We suggest that new professionals set long-range as well as mid-range (5-10 years) and short-term (1-5 years) career goals and audit themselves on a regular basis. Such an audit not only evaluates progress toward specific goals but also the continued appropriateness of the goals. Substituting alternate goals or reconceptualizing time frames may both be in order if progress has not met expectations. Mentors and supervisors are helpful resources in this process, and career counseling may also be desirable for professionals who wish more detailed attention or have continuing concerns about their careers.

Systematic attention to career advancement may well be the key. Financial advisors recommend calculating a net worth statement as part of annual tax preparation, and manufacturers of smoke detectors recommend replacing old batteries twice a year when clocks are adjusted for daylight savings time. An opportune time for career auditing may be around the time of annual performance appraisals and/or salary adjustment meetings. However, in light of Winston and Creamer's (1997) finding that sizeable proportions of student affairs directors (37%) and coordinators (27%) received no formal performance appraisal in a 12-month period, many new professionals may need to select another marker event to trigger a yearly career audit. Denzine's (2001) approach of creating professional portfolios as part of ongoing staff development could be tailored to one's individual needs to provide cumulative documentation of accomplishments, competencies, and growth in a format that can guide and prompt further development.

In addition to reflecting about specific job responsibilities, professionals should ask themselves typical questions such as "What am I good at?" and "What do I enjoy?" Hillman (cited in Perry, 1997) suggested contemplating what the world or other people seem to need or want from us as a complementary way of gaining self-knowledge. New professionals should also address the following questions regularly: "What are my contributions to students, staff, and the campus?" "Am I satisfied and successful with what I am doing?" "Am I able to do the work I want to in this setting?" "Am I accepted and validated as a professional and a person?" "What are my opportunities for further growth?" "What do I want to do next?" "What has changed in my life during the past year, and how do I respond to that?"

Your own answers to these questions will ideally be supplemented with performance appraisal feedback, but these questions can also help identify your accomplishments, your promise, and your commitments. Of course, these answers may change as new staff, colleagues, and supervisors depart campus or arrive, and as work settings are reconfigured. Because of these professional and personal changes, your answers may be different even from one year to the next. Setting goals and addressing these questions help you evaluate regularly the fit with your current position as well as progress on your identified career path.

In general, we suggest the following activities as beneficial for all professionals in student affairs. Identify your own strengths and acknowledge weaker areas. Seek or create opportunities to demonstrate your strengths and address your weaknesses through professional development activities. Regard yourself as a student as well as a contributor. Seek opportunities to learn from others, and also seek opportunities to teach and help others. Anticipate personal, institutional, and environmental changes and identify the ways in which these changes will have an impact on your stated plans and goals. Identify constraints and opportunities, and be prepared to capitalize on professional opportunities for risk-taking and skill development. Finally, work hard. Student affairs work is challenging but also rewarding and, at times, exhilarating. As one student affairs professional wryly remarked, "I don't get a high salary, but that's not why I'm in this line of work. I'm in it for the cards," referring to holiday cards and letters she receives from current and former students and staff members. Our work as educators, advocates, counselors, and life-long learners provides its own personal and career rewards to those who value the satisfaction of working with students and having an impact on their lives.

REFERENCES

Allen, K. E. (1987). Six stages of competence. National Association of Campus Activities (Ed.), *Future perfect: A guide for professional development and competence* (pp. 9-14). Columbia, SC: NACA.

Appleton, J. R., Briggs, C. M., & Rhatigan, J. J. (1978). *Pieces of eight: The rites, roles, and styles of the dean by eight who have been there.* Portland, OR: NASPA Institute for Research and Development.

Belch, H. A., & Strange, C. C. (1995). Views from the bottleneck: Middle managers in student affairs. *NASPA Journal, 32,* 208-222.

Berwick, K. R. (1992). Stress among student affairs administrators: The relationship of personal characteristics and organizational variables of work-related stress. *Journal of College Student Development, 33,* 11-19.

Birch, E. (1984). Thoughts on career advancement. In A. F. Kirby & D. Woodard (Eds.), *Career perspectives in student affairs* (NASPA Monograph Series, Vol. 1., pp. 43-52). Washington, DC: National Association of Student Personnel Administrators.

Brown, R. D., Podolske, D. L., Kohles, R. D., & Sonnenberg, R. L. (1992). Becoming a reflective student affairs administrator. *NASPA Journal, 29*, 307-314.

Burkhalter, J. P. (1984). *Career patterns of chief student personnel administrators.* (Unpublished doctoral dissertation, University of Georgia, Athens, 1984). *Dissertations Abstracts International, 45*, A0425.

Burns, M. (1982). Who leaves the student development field? *NASPA Journal, 20*, 9-12.

Denzine, G. (2001). Making a commitment to professional growth: Realizing the potential of professional portfolios. *NASPA Journal, 38*(4), 495-509.

Derr, C. B. (1986). *Managing the new careerists: The diverse career success orientations of today's workers.* San Francisco: Jossey-Bass.

Dewey, J. (1926). *Democracy and education.* NY: Macmillan.

Evans, N. J. (1988). Attrition of student affairs professionals: A review of the literature. *Journal of College Student Development, 29*(1), 19-24.

Fey, C. J., & Carpenter, D. S. (1996). Mid-level student affairs administrators: Management skills and professional development needs. *NASPA Journal, 33*, 218-231.

Gordon, S. E., Strode, C. B., & Mann, B. A. (1993). The mid-manager in student affairs: What are CSAOs looking for? *NASPA Journal, 30*, 290-297.

Holmes, D., Verrier, D., & Chisholm, P. (1983). Persistence in student affairs work: Attitudes and job shifts among master's program graduates. *Journal of College Student Personnel, 24*, 438-443.

Janasiewicz, B. A., & Wright, D. L. (1993). Job market trends in student affairs: Ten years later. *NASPA Journal, 30*, 145-152.

Kauffman, J. F. (1983). Commentary on examining the myths of administrative careers. *ASHE Bulletin, 35*, 7-8.

Komives, S. R. (1993). Advancing professionally through graduate education. In M. J. Barr & Associates, *The handbook of student affairs administration* (pp. 390-411). San Francisco: Jossey-Bass.

Lorden, L. P. (1998). Attrition in the student affairs profession. *NASPA Journal, 35*(3), 207-216.

Lovell, C. D., & Kosten, L. A. (2000). Skills, knowledge, and personal traits necessary for success as a student affairs administrator: A meta-analysis of thirty years of research. *NASPA Journal, 37*(4), 553-572.

Lunsford, L. W. (1984). Chief student affairs officer: The ladder to the top. *NASPA Journal, 22,* 48-56.

Manning, K. (1994). Liberation theology and student affairs. *Journal of College Student Development, 35,* 94-97.

Miner, A. S., & Estler, S. E. (1985). Accrual mobility: Job mobility in higher education through responsibility accrual. *Journal of Higher Education, 56,* 121-143.

Moore, K. M. (1984). The structure of administrative careers: A prose poem in four parts. *Review of Higher Education, 8*(1), 1-13.

Nobbe, J., & Manning, S. (1997). Issues for women in student affairs with children. *NASPA Journal, 34,* 101-111.

O'Banion, T. (1997). *A learning college for the 21st century.* Phoenix, AZ: Oryx.

Perry, S. (1997, January-February). Waking up with the house on fire: An interview with James Hillman. *Utne Reader,* 53-55.

Rames, M. P. (2000). Effect of financial constraints on student affairs services. *NASPA Journal, 38*(1), 70-81.

Rhatigan, J. J. (1996). Simple gifts: Reflections on the profession. *NASPA Journal, 34,* 67-77.

Rhoads, R. A., & Black, M. A. (1995). Student affairs practitioners as transformative educators: Advancing a critical cultural perspective. *Journal of College Student Development, 36,* 413-421.

Richmond, J., & Sherman, K. J. (1991). Student-development preparation and placement: A longitudinal study of graduate students' and new professionals' experiences. *Journal of College Student Development, 32,* 8-16.

Richmond, J., & Benton, S. (1988). Student affairs graduates' anticipated and actual placement plans. *Journal of College Student Development, 29,* 119-124.

Rickard, S. T. (1985). The chief student affairs officer: Progress toward equity. *Journal of College Student Personnel, 26,* 5-10.

Robinson, D. C., & Delbridge-Parker, L. (1991). A model job rotation plan: A 10-year follow-up. *NASPA Journal, 28,* 172-178.

Sagaria, M. A. D., & Dickens, C. S. (1990). Thriving at home: Developing a career as an insider. In K. M. Moore & S. B. Twombley (Eds.), *Administrative careers and the marketplace* (New Directions for Higher Education, No. 72, pp. 19-28). San Francisco: Jossey-Bass.

Sagaria, M. A. D., & Johnsrud, L. K. (1988). Mobility within the student affairs profession: Career advancement through position change. *Journal of College Student Development, 29,* 30-40.

Saunders, S. A., & Cooper, D. L. (1999). The doctorate in student affairs: Essential skills and competencies for midmanagement. *Journal of College Student Development, 40*(2), 185-191.

Scher, M., & Barr, M. J. (1979). Beyond graduate school: *Strategies for survival. Journal of College Student Personnel, 20,* 529-533.

Schon, D. A. (1983). *The reflective practitioner: How professionals think in action.* NY: Harper Collins.

Shriberg, A., & Wester, S. R. (1994). Employment satisfaction among non-Catholic student affairs professionals at Catholic colleges and universities. *Journal of College Student Development, 35,* 109-112.

Task Force on Professional Preparation and Practice. (1990). *The recruitment, preparation, and nurturing of the student affairs professional.* Washington, DC: National Association of Student Personnel Administrators.

Townsend, B. K., & Wiese, M. (1992). The value of a doctorate in higher education for student affairs administrators. *NASPA Journal, 30,* 51-58.

Turrentine, C. G., & Conley, V. M. (2001). Two measures of the diversity of the labor pool for entry-level student affairs positions. *NASPA Journal, 39*(1), 84-102.

Twombly, S. B. (1990). Career maps and institutional highways. In K. M. Moore & S. B. Twombley (Eds.), *Administrative careers and the marketplace* (New Directions for Higher Education, No. 72, pp. 5-18). San Francisco: Jossey-Bass.

Van Maanen, J. (1983). Doing new things in old ways: The chains of socialization. In J. L. Bess (Ed.), *College and university organization: Insights from the behavioral sciences.* NY: New York University Press.

Ward, L. (1995). Role stress and propensity to leave among new student affairs professionals. *NASPA Journal, 33*(1), 35-44.

Young, R. B. (1994). Student affairs professionals' perceptions of barriers to participation in development activities. *NASPA Journal, 31,* 243-251.

CHAPTER 9

Words of Wisdom

SHANNON E. ELLIS

*Y*ou have chosen well.

Whether you fell in to the student affairs profession by accident or have methodically studied and planned your career, it does not matter. The exemplary senior student affairs officers who contributed to this chapter shaped successful careers from both origins. Each would concur with Eliseo Torres, Vice President for Student Affairs at the University of New Mexico, who pursued a career both in and out of higher education. "All the years I have worked in student services have been the best years of my life," he says. Senior administrators agree that you are destined for a life full of fascinating people, provocative problems, global exploration, instigating change, deep sadness, and the highest elations—all because you have the daily capacity to create a better world.

Pretty heady stuff, isn't it? But that's exactly what we all do at every level of this profession, on all types of campuses, in all possible places, teaching every imaginable kind of student who is seeking a higher education.

Some have described our profession as a cult. Others subscribe to it like a religion. These extreme and controversial comparisons emphasize the deep passion and total commitment that student affairs professionals feel toward their students, their campuses, and their work. We are clearly fortunate to have found a career that offers these challenges and this satisfaction. It is hard to imagine writing such words about many other career paths. It is harder still to imagine working in another field. When you find the work you enjoy, at which you excel, that pays the bills, and that, most days, doesn't even feel like a job, then you know it is something extra special that will create for you a fulfilling life.

You may already have experienced what so many senior student affairs officers consider to be the rewards of this profession. In Eliseo Torres' words: "Sometimes I receive notes, e-mails, phone calls, and letters from former students thanking me for making a positive change in their lives and every time I receive these messages, I am reminded how fortunate I am to work with these wonderful people."

FOCUS ON MAKING A DIFFERENCE...EVEN WHEN YOU DON'T THINK YOU ARE.

Barbara Hollmann, Vice President for Student Affairs at the University of Montana, Missoula, elaborates: "We want our efforts to make a difference, but we may not realize how our actions and decisions are being perceived or what effect they are having. We are role models whether we want to be or not. Visits with former students recall times that we may have forgotten, but which made a great impact on the student's life." It is often the small actions taken that are the most significant, not the highly visible events that we think make a difference in the lives of students. Don't let this scare you. Rather, be inspired by it!

IT IS EASY TO BE A SUPERVISOR, BUT NOT SO EASY TO BE A GREAT SUPERVISOR.

Students are not the only ones looking to you for guidance. Staff members seek a similar kind of direction from you as your career offers more opportunities to supervise. Almeda Jacks, Vice President for Student Affairs at Clemson University, is as inspired to cultivate excellent professionals on her staff as she is to serve students. If not, she says, "supervision becomes a chore. Take on the role of facilitator to allow a team—your team—to be successful." Jacks inspires herself and her staff by ensuring their success through clear and obtainable objectives. This motivates her to go to bat for salaries and promotions that are well-documented and well-deserved. Such actions ensure that she will be a strong supervisor, manager, and leader. All these roles, she stresses, are important. Trust is a critical component to creating an effective team, which Jacks instills with a policy of "no secrets." This includes everything from open budgets and open policies to open communication. It is further strengthened by performance evaluation that goes up and down. Always welcome input and feedback and keep the flow going both ways. And finally, for students, faculty, and staff, lead by example in every way.

HOW YOU PROCESS SOMETHING IS JUST AS IMPORTANT AS THE SUBSTANCE OF WHAT YOU ARE TRYING TO WIN SUPPORT FOR.

George Wallman, Vice President for Student Affairs at North Dakota State University, provides a lesson in leading by example from his own administrative journey. "Process to me is interpersonal communication," he says. "It involves listening, a willingness to compromise, and being willing to take the time to let others react. Nothing tends to generate resistance more than the perception that you are on a fast track with something and it will be forced on people immediately." Wallman further emphasizes the role of understanding opposition, stating: "In processing an idea, we need to be careful not to create personal opposition when all the person was against was the substance of what we were presenting. We can have people who are against our idea and we can have people who just plain don't like us as individuals."

HAVE BROAD SHOULDERS AND SMALL TEAR DUCTS.

There is no doubt about it. This can be a tough profession. Critics, controversy, public tensions, and endless problems face a student affairs professional each day. Perhaps that is exactly why we love this work. The ability to develop skills that allow us to lead the campus in creating a positive environment for student learning comes with experience. Do not fool yourself. Even the best student affairs professionals make mistakes. But they learn from them by reflecting, evaluating, and accepting constructive feedback and criticism from others. Thick skin, a commitment to the bigger picture, and a self-assurance that allows for improvement will not only sustain a successful career in this field; it will ensure it. Clearly, Dick McKaig, Vice President for Student Affairs at Indiana University-Bloomington, is right when he says, "Student affairs is not for the weak of heart or the insecure." What makes all the difference for a rewarding career in student affairs is "institutional fit."

BE SURE YOU UNDERSTAND AND RESPECT THE MISSION OF THE INSTITUTION WHERE YOU WORK.

In fact, be motivated by it. "Institutional fit" makes all the difference for a fulfilling career in student affairs. McKaig explains, "In student affairs, you can be a change agent, but you start in a context that is set by the history, tradition, and mission of the institution." Select an institution that is a good fit for you and one that you can fully embrace. Don't try to make your institution be what it wasn't intended to be. Participate in and benefit from the best of what it is and accept the problems. Use language that is valued and understood by your on-campus audience and avoid student affairs jargon. Often this means finding the words of academicians.

STAY LEARNER-CENTERED.

Staying "student-centered" is the senior student affairs administrator's way of saying, "Be completely connected to the academic mission of your institution." Mary Olson, Vice President for Student Affairs at Oakton Community College, reminds us that colleges are about teaching and learning. "It helps if we use the language that is respected by academicians and if we convey our message in few words," she says. "It is also wise to listen more than to tell but, having said that, we shouldn't discount the wisdom we have that faculty colleagues want and need." Totally embrace the student services mission, which is to help students learn. Everything you do is about helping students have the best educational experience possible.

BE A STUDENT OF STUDENTS.

No one should know your students better than you. Your ability to understand the demographics, attitudes, trends, and pending changes, and to make predictions for the campus makes you an invaluable asset to the institution. This is only true, however, if you openly share the results of your studies on widespread and regular occasions. Your ability to share the knowledge of your students will greatly increase the impact of successful pedagogy, satisfaction with services, and student learning. Keeping this information a secret or as some false sense of power is a disservice to students and a career-ending strategy.

BE A PROBLEM-SOLVER, NOT STARTER.

Solve the problems we hope an organized community can solve on campus. Meaning is found in many parts of our work. The ability to bring people together to resolve issues is extremely satisfying. The senior student affairs officers contributing to this chapter stressed the need to make yourself indispensable to the institution. Be sure that, if you and your program disappeared tomorrow, the college or university would fall apart. By sharing what you know about students, by facilitating conversations about the implications of pedagogy or budget allocations, you lead the community in becoming one that curbs substance abuse and violence, that retains students, and that makes students smarter as they learn.

RESPECT THE HISTORICAL PERSPECTIVE OF CAMPUS COLLEAGUES.

Art Costantino, Vice President of Student Affairs at Evergreen State College, likens the arrival of new staff on campus to the tension between the enduring influence of past circumstances on world events and U.S. foreign policy that seeks a "quick fix" to century-old disputes. "An analogous situation occurs when a new staff member arrives on campus," he explains. "The newcomer will be working with colleagues who remember events from the past and who have a long-term view of the college. It can be frustrating to be told that an idea will not work based on something that occurred ten years ago, but to be successful, new staff members should convey respect for the past and strive to understand the perspectives of those who have a protracted view of time." If you are promoting an idea that has been tried before, not only will you need to be sensitive to the past; you will also need to be persuasive about why past conditions no longer apply.

> No one should know your students better than you. Your ability to understand the demographics, attitudes, trends and pending changes, and to make predictions for the campus makes you an invaluable asset to the institution.

144

IDENTIFY AND DEVELOP PRINCIPLES TO DIRECT YOUR LIFE.

Mary Olson adds, "I think it is essential that student affairs people know who they are and what they are about and that there be consistency between our private and public selves. I've been fortunate to be in a professional position and at an institution that allows me to be who I am."

Olson should know. She was 32 years old when she went to work at Oakton and the community college was only three years old. Their shared youth allowed them to grow together and shape one another. Upon reflection she says, "Many colleges give you a flight plan...Oakton gave me wings to fly. I have come to love this place."

IF YOU CAN'T LOVE WHERE YOU ARE AND RESPECT YOUR STUDENTS, FIND ANOTHER PLACE WHERE YOU CAN.

"To do that," Olson advises, "you need to know what helps you flourish and what inhibits you or makes you feel conflicted. Know what you can change and what you can adapt to and, if you are in a situation that won't work, leave it." This does not, however, preclude being an agent of change at your institution. All senior student affairs officer have made major changes in the higher education institutions where they have worked by improving services and programs to students.

ADVOCATE FOR STUDENT INTERESTS, BUT DON'T USE YOUR ROLE AS A STUDENT ADVOCATE TO PURSUE YOUR PERSONAL AGENDAS.

Art Costantino has found that student advocacy requires careful representation of the concerns of individual students and groups of students. "You should strive to make it clear whether you are trying to reflect what students are saying or whether you are talking about what you believe is in the best interest of students," he advises. "Whatever you do, try not to project your beliefs or agenda onto students." Dick McKaig adds, "The needs of students will change over your student affairs career. It is more important to know how to assess student needs and facilitate change than it is to understand what you and your peers wanted as students."

KEEP YOUR EYE ON THE HORIZON...EVEN WHEN WORKING IN THE TRENCHES.

Change is necessary to avoid becoming obsolete, or at best, stale. Barbara Hollmann stresses that, "As a young professional, you want to be assured that there will be jobs as you advance in your career. Student affairs as a profession will change...or become obsolete. As higher education evolves, so must student affairs. Lift your eyes from the trenches from time to time and view your work from perspectives outside student affairs and towards the future." Peggy Jablonski, Dean of Student Life at Brown University, encourages visiting the work of student affairs from the perspective of another country by participating in a study tour sponsored by a professional association or by putting together one of your own.

With change and the future in mind, Eliseo Torres states that one of the best programs to encourage people of color to explore the field is NASPA's Minority Undergraduate Fellows Program. This is another example of the importance of active membership in professional associations for student affairs.

SEEK AFFILIATION WITH PROFESSIONAL ORGANIZATIONS SUCH AS NASPA TO CULTIVATE SKILLS, DEVELOP NETWORKS OF COLLEAGUES, AND REINFORCE ETHICS.

Like all of the senior student affairs officers contributing their perspectives, Peggy Jablonski's professional involvement has led to a personal network of dozens of colleagues from across the country who are valuable resources for advice on professional issues, as well as for job referrals and recommendations. "These wise mentors provide advice and serve as role models to me," she adds.

In addition, do not consider professional activities as just a "fringe" to getting ahead. The myth still exists that you get ahead simply by doing your job and that things like professional involvement are the cream. You want to be professionally active because that is HOW you can do your job well. Solutions to problems, development of new skills, forecasting issues, job contacts, mentors, leadership opportunities, models of best practice, and much more await the student affairs professional who seeks to take advantage of all associations have to offer.

PERIODICALLY REVIEW PROFESSIONAL STANDARDS AND ETHICAL CODES.

Each fall, Art Costantino meets with new staff in student affairs on his campus. As part of the process, they review codes of ethics and statements regarding good practice, such as the American College Personnel Association's "Statement of Ethical Principles and Standards," NASPA's "Principles of Good Practice for Student Affairs," and the Guidelines of the Council for the Advancement of Standards for Student Affairs Programs. "Become familiar with these documents," Costantino says. "They reflect the judgment of experienced professionals and are helpful guidelines regarding best practices."

CLAIM THE CAMPUS AS YOUR SPACE.

The responsibility to ensure that students have an exceptional educational experience on your campus demands such a belief. "Maintain appropriate and respectful personal boundaries," warns Mary Olson. "Most of the trouble we get into is when we violate boundaries of one sort or another." Having said this, she encourages us to "show up in unexpected places to see people and act as if you belong there."

Professional development encompasses clear values, broad capabilities, and valuable work experiences. Senior student affairs officers stress the need to:

• Follow through on commitments.
• Avoid self-promotion. It gets old!
• Become a good writer by rewriting until it is right.
• Always arrive prepared.
• Think hard before saying "no" to a request or an assignment.
• Seize opportunities to learn and demonstrate new qualities.
• Teach if you are qualified.
• Develop trust.
• Learn to distinguish the urgent from the important…the useful from the useless.
• Create a context for the work you are doing so you see its larger purpose

All senior student affairs officers were new professionals once. While it was a long time ago, we all remember it as a time of great fun, when we knew everything and nothing, tried to listen and learn from those more senior while forging our way with new ideas and fresh approaches, reading everything in the field, and feeling fortunate to attend student affairs institutes and conferences. We quickly learned that all the cutting edge knowledge gained in our graduate programs, if we were even in a college student development program, served us well for close to the next five years, but by then the learning cycle needed to be rejuvenated forever.

BEND RULES AND GET RID OF THE DUMB ONES.

Many recall thinking that, when they achieved certain responsibilities in the field, they would change things. And they have. Their advice is to bend the rules. It is a great joy to realize that, because we make the policies and rules, we can change them. It is motivating to answer the question, "If we were truly student-centered, what would this campus be like?" with acts of real change led by speedy and strategic thinking. We are inspired by staff, faculty, and students who not only raise the question but also bring resolutions.

NEW PROFESSIONALS FRESH FROM GRADUATE PROGRAMS SHOULD RECOGNIZE THE DIFFERENCES BETWEEN THE CLASSROOM AND WORK SETTINGS AND RELISH THE COMPLEXITY OF THE WORKPLACE.

At some point, we became aware of the difference between the classroom setting and the work setting. Costantino reminds us that a classroom is not a workplace. "In a classroom, the participants come together for relatively short periods of time, arguments tend to be based on reason, and alternative courses of action can be contemplated without the pressure to make an actual decision," he says. "In a workplace, individuals have often worked together for years and have developed fascinating patterns of influence and connection. The rational and irrational are mixed, and it is often necessary to quickly arrive at a single course of action." Despite this, no matter what you do in student affairs, be it entry, mid or senior level work, your parents will never understand your job and profession. So ignore it and...

ENJOY YOUR LIFE. WORK ISN'T EVERYTHING.

Barbara Hollmann reminds us that working in student affairs can consume our lives if we allow it. Avoid burnout by balancing personal time and professional time. Take time for professional development and renewal within your professional lives. Learn to say no when professional commitments creep into private time. Hollmann summarizes that, "A long career in student affairs demands energy, enthusiasm, and commitment, which can be retained only through a healthy balance of caring for one's self and nurturing one's career." Just as you develop a vision for your organization, so should you craft a vision for your own personal and professional journey.

SET AN AGENDA FOR YOURSELF.

Develop a vision of "the possible." Make this vision congruent with the vision of senior campus administrators. Make this vision an incorporation of current and future thinking.

Develop a vision of "the possible." Make this vision congruent with the vision of senior campus administrators. Make this vision an incorporation of current and future thinking. Make this vision a long look into the future – the future of college students, of higher education, of the student affairs profession, and, most of all, of you. Create and promote this vision so that at first it becomes possible and then, eventually, a reality. Think of yourself and everyone else as a resource in developing competencies and personal influence. Adopt the right mindset, participate willingly, build success for others, and model personal and professional development by leading with integrity.

Concluding insights

What kind of student affairs professional will you become? What values will you hold and act upon in this profession as you compose yourself?

We offer some concluding inspirations that should confirm your choice to spend a life in service to students, learning, and higher education:

- Look into a student's eyes when you are listening.
- Walk up and introduce yourself to the scariest faculty member on campus.
- Replace your youth with mystery.
- Stop in the middle of the craziest part of the day and admire a piece of art.
- Read your NASPA Journal when it arrives instead of tossing it into a pile.
- Find a handful of colleagues along the way to whom you can turn with your problems and worries for honest advice, sympathy, and friendship.
- Let students and new professionals hang around you—create opportunities for them to learn.
- Change lives, lots of lives, every single day.
- Cry when a student tells you he or she is a heroin addict or a survivor of incest or has been abused by his/her partner.
- Celebrate when a student is six months into recovery, living in a shelter, getting a "B" in statistics.
- Change yourself because of their tragedies and achievements.
- Be funny...make people laugh; put them at ease.
- Read each college generation's version of Rolling Stone or Spin magazine; listen to their music; watch MTV once in a while and ask students what they like on TV, at the movies, and to read in the summer.
- Struggle with a real life ethical dilemma at least once a day.
- View criticism and negative feedback as "a gift."
- Bring a "Top 10" CD to the office, play it loud after 5 p.m., and dance to it alone.
- Be the one to always ask, "How is this best for our students?"
- Reflect once in a while.
- Travel to foreign lands every year to remember what it is like to be a new student on a strange campus.
- Remember birthdays.
- Help realize dreams.
- ...especially your own.

The inspiration and advice shared by successful senior student affairs officers from a variety of institutions, backgrounds, and beliefs is given to you, the new professional, as a gift. The gift is to learn from our mistakes, be motivated by our insights, and fully embrace the wonderful life you have chosen as a student affairs professional. You will occasionally have your doubts; you will most certainly know failure, conflict, and sadness. Be assured these will easily be outweighed by the triumphs, easy comfort of career fit, your personal commitment, and the realization of dreams—both yours and your students.'

Welcome to the finest profession in the world.

Welcome to our world.

Professional Organizations in Student Affairs and Higher Education

American Association of Collegiate Registrars and Admissions Officers

Acronym:	AACRAO
Category:	Admissions and Student Records/Registrars
National Headquarters:	One Dupont Circle N.W., Suite 520
	Washington, D.C., 20036-1171
	(202) 293-9161, FAX (202) 872-8857
E-mail:	info@aacrao.org
Website:	http://www.aacrao.org

American College Personnel Association

Acronym:	ACPA
Category:	General Student Affairs
National Headquarters:	One Dupont Circle, Suite 300
	Washington D.C. 20036-1110
	(202) 835-ACPA(2272), FAX (202) 296-3286
E-mail:	info@acpa.nche.edu
Website:	http://www.acpa.nche.edu

Association of College Unions International

Acronym:	ACUI
Category:	Student Unions
National Headquarters:	Marsha Herman-Betzen, Executive Director
	One City Centre, Suite 200
	120 W. 7th St., Bloomington, IN 47404-3925
	(812) 855-8550, FAX (812) 855-0162
E-mail:	info@acuiweb.org
Website:	http://acuiweb.org

Association of College and University Housing Officers — International

Acronym:	ACUHO-I
Category:	Student Housing
National Headquarters:	941 Chatham Lane, Suite 318
	Columbus, OH 43201
	(614) 292-0099, FAX (614) 292-3205
E-mail:	osuacuho@postbox.acs.ohio-state.edu
Website:	http://www.acuho.ohio-state.edu

Association of International Educators: NAFSA

Acronym:	NAFSA
Category:	International Students
National Headquarters:	Marlene M. Johnson, Executive Director and CEO
	1307 New York Ave. NW, 8th Floor
	Washington, D.C. 20005
	(202) 737-3699, FAX (202) 737-3657
E-mail:	inbox@nafsa.org
Website:	http://www.nafsa.org

Association of Fraternal Advisors

Acronym:	AFA
Category:	Greek Affairs
National Headquarters:	Sue Kraft Fussell, Executive Director
	3901 W. 86th Street, Suite 165
	Indianapolis, IN 46268-1702
	(317) 876-1632, FAX (317) 876-3981
E-mail:	info@fraternityadvisors.org
Website:	http://www.fraternityadvisors.org

American Association for Employment in Education

Acronym:	AAEE
Category:	Placement Services for Education Majors
National Headquarters:	B. J. Bryant, Executive Director
	3049 Riverside Drive, Suite 125
	Columbus, OH 43221
	(614) 485-1111, FAX (614) 485-9609
E-mail:	aaee@osu.edu
Website:	http://www.aaee.org

Association for the Study of Higher Education

Acronym:	ASHE
Category:	Higher Education Faculty and Administrators
National Headquarters:	Barbara K. Townsend, Executive Director
	202 Hill Hall
	University of Missouri-Columbia
	Columbia, MO 65211-2190
	(573) 882-9645, FAX (573) 884-2197
E-mail:	ashe@tiger.coe.missouri.edu
Website:	http://www.coe.missouri.edu/~ashe

Association for Student Judicial Affairs

Acronym:	ASJA
Category:	Student Judicial Affairs
National Headquarters:	P.O. Box 2237
	College Station, TX 77841-2237
	(979) 845-5262, FAX (979) 458-1714
E-mail:	asja@tamu.edu
Website:	http://asja.tamu.edu/

National Academic Advising Association

Acronym:	NACADA
Category:	Academic Advising
National Headquarters:	Bobbie Flaherty, Executive Director
	Kansas State University
	2323 Anderson Ave., Suite 225
	Manhattan, Kansas 66502-2912
	(785) 532-5717, FAX (785) 532-7732
E-mail:	nacada@ksu.edu
Website:	http://www.nakada.ksu.edu

National Association for Campus Activities

Acronym:	NACA
Category:	Student Activities
National Headquarters:	Alan Davis, Executive Director
	13 Harbison Way
	Columbia, SC 29212-3401
	(803) 732-6222, FAX (803) 749-1047
E-mail:	aland@dbs.naca.org
Website:	http://www.naca.org

National Association of College Admissions Counselors

Acronym:	NACAC
Category:	Admissions
National Headquarters:	1631 Prince Street
	Alexandria, VA 22314-2818
	(703) 836-2222, FAX (703) 836-8015
E-mail:	Info@nacac.com
Website:	http://www.nacac.com/Index.html

National Association of Colleges and Employers

Acronym:	NACE
Category:	Placement
National Headquarters:	Marilyn F. Mackes, Executive Director
	62 Highland Ave.
	Bethlehem, PA 18017
	(610) 868-1421 or 1-800-544-5272
	FAX (610) 868-0208
E-mail:	mmackes@naceweb.org
Website:	http://www.naceweb.org/default.cfm

National Association of College Auxiliary Services

Acronym:	NACAS
Category:	Auxiliary Services
National Headquarters:	Jeff Perdue, Interim Executive Director
	7 Boar's Head Lane
	Charlottesville, VA 22903-4610
	(434) 245-8425, FAX (434) 245-8453
E-mail:	nacas@cfw.com
Website:	http://www.nacas.org

National Association of Student Financial Aid Administrators

Acronym:	NASFAA
Category:	Financial Aid
National Headquarters:	Dallas Martin, Executive Officio.
	1129 20th Street, NW, Suite 400
	Washington, D.C. 20036
	(202) 785-0453, FAX (202) 785-1487
E-mail:	ask@nasfaa.org
Website:	http://www.nasfaa.org

National Association of Student Personnel Administrators

Acronym:	NASPA
Category:	General Student Affairs
National Headquarters:	1875 Connecticut Ave. N.W., Suite 418
	Washington, D.C. 20009-5728
	(202) 265-7500, FAX (202) 797-1157
E-mail:	office@naspa.org
Website:	http://www.naspa.org

National Orientation Directors Association

Acronym:	NODA
Category:	Orientation Staff and Directors
National Headquarters:	Washington State University
	Office of New Student Programs
	PO Box 641070
	Pullman, WA 99164-1070
	(509) 335-6459, FAX (509) 335-2078
E-mail:	noda@nodaweb.org
Website:	http://www.nodaweb.org/

NASPA

Monograph Contributors

MARILYN J. AMEY is Associate Professor of Higher Education at Michigan State University. Marilyn received her bachelor's degree in Elementary and Special Education from Wittenberg University, a master's degree in College Student Personnel from The Ohio State University, and a Ph.D. in Higher Education from Penn State University. Previously, she was a faculty member at the University of Kansas, and she has student affairs experience in residence life and student activities. She is a member of the inaugural class of NASPA Faculty Fellows.

CAMILLE CONSOLVO is the Assistant to the Vice President for Student Affairs at Bowling Green State University. She received her Ph.D. in counseling psychology at Florida State University and her bachelor's and master's degrees from Southwest Missouri State University. She has worked in counseling, career services, orientation, judicial affairs, disability services, and leadership development, and has held several administrative positions in both student affairs and academic affairs.

MICHAEL DANNELLS is Professor and Director of the Higher Education Administration Ph.D. program at Bowling Green State University in Ohio. He received his Ph.D. in College Student Development and Higher Education from the University of Iowa and his bachelor's degree from Bradley University. Previously, he was a faculty member at Kansas State University, and his practitioner experience includes student life, residence life, and new student programs.

SHANNON E. ELLIS is Vice President of Student Services at the University of Nevada, Reno. She received her Ph.D. in Higher Education from the University of Southern California, her master's in Public Administration from the University of Massachusetts-Amherst and her Bachelor of Science in Journalism from the University of Illinois-Champaign Urbana. Shannon is a past president of the National Association of Student Personnel Administrators (NASPA).

KELLY A. GRADY is a Higher Education doctoral student and research assistant at the University of Pennsylvania. She earned a B.A. in psychology from the University of Maryland and an M.Ed. in Higher Education and Student Affairs from the University of Vermont. Kelly worked several years in residence life and in first year student programs before returning to school full time.

DAVID S. GUTHRIE is the Director/Professor of the Master's in Higher Education Program at Geneva College. He holds a Ph.D. in Higher Education from Penn State University, a master's degree in Religion from Pittsburgh Theological Seminary, and a bachelor's degree in Sociology and Religion from Grove City College. Dave was formerly the Dean of Student Development and Adjunct Assistant Professor of Sociology at Calvin College.

FLORENCE A. HAMRICK is Associate Professor of Higher Education at Iowa State University. She received her bachelor's degree in English from the University of North Carolina at Chapel Hill, her master's degree in College Student Personnel from The Ohio State University, and her Ph.D. in Higher Education from Indiana University. Flo worked in residence life and career services and also served as the national chair for the NASPA New Professionals Network.

BRIAN O. HEMPHILL is the Associate Vice Chancellor for Student Affairs and Dean of Students at the University of Arkansas. He earned his B.A. in Organizational Communications at St. Augustine's College, M.S. in Journalism and Mass Communications at Iowa State University, and his Ph.D. in Higher Education Administration at the University of Iowa. Brian previously worked at Iowa State University, Cornell College, and the University of North Carolina at Wilmington. He currently serves as the National Coordinator for the NASPA Minority Undergraduate Fellows Program.

LORI McDONALD is currently the Assistant Dean of Students and Greek Advisor at the University of Utah. She received her B.S. in Biology from the University of Utah and then earned her M.A. in Higher Education and Student Affairs from The Ohio State University. She has previous experience in academic advising and career services.

THOMAS E. McWHERTOR is the Vice President for Enrollment and External Relations at Calvin College. Formerly the Director of Admissions at Calvin, his extensive postsecondary experience prior to Calvin spans student activities, residence life, public relations, and campus ministry. He received his Master of Divinity from Gordon-Conwell Theological Seminary. Tom has also worked in government and public relations in Washington, D.C., and has served as a communications and special events consultant with various non-profit organizations.

LORI M. REESOR is currently an Assistant Dean in the School of Education at the University of Missouri Kansas City. Lori received her bachelor's degree from the University of Wisconsin-Whitewater, her master's in Higher Education from Iowa State University, and her doctorate in Educational Policy and Leadership from the University of Kansas. She is the former Dean of Students at Wichita State University and worked in residence life, orientation, and admissions at the University of Kansas. She is a former NASPA Regional Vice President for Region IV-West.

RANDI S. SCHNEIDER has a bachelor's degree in Social Work, a master's in Counselor Education from Illinois State University, and her doctorate from the University of Illinois at Urbana-Champaign. Currently, Randi is the Director of the Student Health Center at Indiana University of Pennsylvania. Randi's student affairs experience has been in residential life, health services, student activities, and student services.

BARBARA SNYDER is the Vice President for Student Affairs at the University of Utah. She received her bachelor's degree at The Ohio State University in Home Economics/Speech Communication, her master's degree from St. Cloud State University in Counseling, and her Ph.D. in Higher Education from Iowa State University. Previously, she served as Vice Chancellor for Student Affairs at the University of Nebraska at Kearney.

J. DOUGLAS TOMA teaches higher education management at the University of Pennsylvania, Graduate School of Education, where he established and now directs The Executive Doctorate. He earned his Ph.D. in higher education, M.A. in history, and J.D., all from the University of Michigan, and his B.A. in history and public policy from Michigan State University.

Printed in the United States
136761LV00007B/11/P